AT THE GATES OF DAWN

A COLLECTION OF WRITINGS BY ELLA YOUNG

edited by

John Matthews and Denise Sallee

SKYLIGHT PRESS

First published in Great Britain in 2011 by Skylight Press,
210 Brooklyn Road, Cheltenham, Glos GL51 8EA

Designed and typeset by Rebsie Fairholm
Printed and bound in Great Britain by Lightning Source, Milton Keynes

www.skylightpress.co.uk

ISBN 978-1-908011-16-9

CONTENTS

Poems from THE ROSE OF HEAVEN and TO THE LITTLE PRINCESS: AN EPISTLE

Stories from CELTIC WONDER TALES

Poems from SMOKE OF MYRRH

Stories from THE TANGLE-COATED HORSE

PART TWO: AUTOBIOGRAPHY AND OTHER WRITINGS

ACKNOWLEDGEMENTS

Cover artwork: Portrait of Ella Young Seated in a Garden by Maud Lloyd. Courtesy of The Bancroft Library, University of California, Berkeley.

p.10: Ella Young's Faculty Portrait, University of California, Berkeley. No date. Photograph by Kee Coleman. Courtesy of The Bancroft Library, University of California, Berkeley.

p.49: Ella Young's Sacred Mount Shasta, 2006. Photograph by Peter Reichelt Hughes. Courtesy of Denise Sallee.

p.79: Portrait of Ella Young (standing by a tree)/Clara E. Sipprell Papers, Special Collections Research Center, Syracuse University Library.

p.133: Ella Young, In Her Garden, Oceano, California, no date. Photograph by Ansel Adams. © 2011 The Ansel Adams Publishing Rights Trust.

p.190: Ella Young with friend artist John O'Shea. Monterey Peninsula, California. No date. Courtesy of Mrs Molly A. Jeppson.

p.210: Ella Young's cottage in Oceano, California, 2007. Photograph by Denise Sallee.

Flowering Dusk: Things Remembered Accurately And Inaccurately by Ella Young, copyright 1945 by Ella Young, renewed 1973 by Jane R. Thompson. Reproduced by permission of Random House, Inc.

Faerie Music diary reproduced by permission of The Huntington Library, San Marino, California. Ella Young Papers. Diary, 1917-1918.

Excerpts from *The Irish Review* reproduced courtesy of the National Library of Ireland.

I would like to thank colleagues who have eased my way into Ella Young's collections of papers and manuscripts on both sides of the Atlantic. First, Simon Elliott, Manuscript Division, Charles E. Young Research Library, Department of Special Collections, UCLA for answering my endless questions; Peter Whidden, Rare Books Specialist, Special Collections & University Archives, Stanford University for helping me to access Ella's rare publications; Nicolette A. Dobrowolski, Reference and Access Services Librarian, Special Collections Research Centre, Syracuse University Library in New York and Fintan Quinn, Assistant Keeper II, National Library of Ireland, Dublin for helping me to tie up loose ends.

In particular, I would like to thank Dr. Kathryn Klar, Lecturer, Celtic Studies, University of California, Berkeley for so generously sharing with me her research on Ella Young, and my friend Mara Freeman, for passing on Ella's torch.

And, finally, I wish to express my deep appreciation to John Matthews for recognizing the spirit of Ella Young and for doing so much to encourage my research. Your belief in me and in Ella has been my beacon.

Denise Sallee, Pacific Grove CA., USA, 2010

I would like to thank Skylight Press for believing in this project, and my co-editor Denise Sallee for generously sharing both the vision and her collection of Ella Young documents and books.

John Matthews, Oxford, UK, 2010

FOREWORD

You only have to look at the photographs of Ella Young within this book to realise that we have a formidable woman here. There is something clear and uncompromising in her eyes – eyes that have seen further and deeper into the unseen worlds than most of us would care to peer.

And as if that were not enough, cast an eye on certain elements in her biography. Born in what is now Northern Ireland of a Protestant family before the troubled island was partitioned, but throwing in her lot with the Republican movement in the south to the extent of gun running in support of the Easter Rising of 1916. An unlikely role for a middle aged member of the Hermetic Society (Dublin branch of the Theosophical Society), protégé of the mystic George Russell and author of a slim volume of *Poems* (in 1906), another on Irish folklore (*The Coming of Lugh*) in 1909, and book of *Celtic Wonder Tales* (1910).

Above all, the strength and integrity of the woman comes out through her writings, much of which are reproduced in this book. Whether stories for children (that would do adults a power of good to read), her poetry, or her re-telling of the myths and legends of the great gods and faeries and heroes of Ireland.

Having had enough of a divided Ireland, in the 1920s she emigrated to America to become a lecturer in Celtic studies at the University of California, Berkeley, where she became a colourful figure, dressed in Druid robes, expounding the lore of faeries, elves and pixies with an authority that seemed to have come from first hand experience as much as academic learning.

Indeed, it is said that because of her frank and fearless views on these matters that she had some trouble being admitted to the United States, which to hard-boiled immigration officials on Ellis Island seemed grounds for banning her on grounds of mental deficiency.

However she was no fey member of a lunatic fringe. Having attained a Masters' degree at the Royal University, Dublin she had learned Gaelic, and spent years in remote areas of Ireland gathering local traditions and lore; she was a forerunner of the American scholar W. Y. Evans-Wentz whose *Fairy Faith in Celtic Countries* she later reviewed. Only with her, much of the research and evidence came at first hand. Witness her diary notes on hearing faery music on the side of Maulin Mountain in County Wicklow between August the 20th 1917 and February 12th 1918.

Any who have trodden the highways and byways of faery with more than a superficial intellectual curiosity will know some of the rewards that this can bring. It includes a new vision and awareness of the vibrancy and intelligent life in all nature, including an especial affinity with trees. And toward the end of her life Ella Young was no less than a friend of the great California Redwoods. Her ashes, at the end of a long and fruitful life, were scattered in a redwood grove.

She was also aware of the power of the hollow hills, and her reverence for the sacred mountain of Shasta, oddly enough, was reflected by Evans-Wentz, who after spending most of his life researching Tibetan mysticism, returned to California to realise the importance of Mount Shasta, virtually in his own back yard.

How can we ourselves make some approach to the reality and vitality of these hidden kingdoms of which Ella Young was an intrepid explorer? She has, as you may discover in these pages, left us a virtual guide book – along with the priceless stimulus of her own enthusiasm to rekindle ancient lights.

For an introduction to the vitality of ancient Irish legend what better stimulus than the beginning of her story that is a virtual Celtic creation myth, with all the gods assembling:

In Tir-na-Moe, the Land of the Living Heart, Brigit was singing. Angus the Ever-Young, and Midyr the Red-Maned, and Ogma that is called Splendour of the Sun, and the Dagda and other lords of the people of Dana drew near to listen.

Thanks to Ella Young, we can draw near to listen too.

Or how better to light the blue touch paper of interior fireworks than the evocation of the moment when:

Nuada, Wielder of the White Light, set up the Spear of Victory in the centre of Ireland. It was like a great fiery fountain. It was like a singing flame.

As she remarked in an interview for *The Oakland Tribune* in 1931: "It's fairy lore that makes the world beautiful ... there are fairies all about us, if we'll only look for them. How sad it is that a materialistic world laughs at them and their beauty ... The fairy kingdom is a vast realm of magic where most anything can happen."

May we, as readers of her work, discover from her something of this lore that makes the world beautiful. Become aware of what is all about us if we will only look. And discover that vast realm where almost anything can happen!

Gareth Knight

Ella Young's Faculty Portrait, University of California, Berkeley. No date.
Photograph by Kee Coleman

ELLA YOUNG
POET OF TRUTH AND BEAUTY

In early Irish society there existed an honoured group of people called the "Filid." They preserved the native stories and they were learned in the magical arts.[1] It is within this ancient tradition that Ella Young (1867-1956) lived her unique and creative life. In the late 1800s Ella began to gather the old tales that had been handed down from family to family for centuries. She lived among the rural folk in the West of Ireland and in the hills south of Dublin. As part of her devotion to Irish culture she learned Gaelic and, as a major contributor to the Celtic Revival, she taught classes in the language and the myths.

Ella's spirituality reached deep into the land and into the heart of ancient Ireland. Others have called her a seeress, a druidess, or a witch – the magical name she gave herself was "Airmid" – the goddess of healing who drew her powers from the fertile green earth. She knew first-hand about the faery folk of Ireland – she heard their music and listened to their stories. Ella was truly blessed – for her life flowed in harmony with her beliefs, her nationalism, and her career as an author and lecturer.

Ella's dear friend Maud Gonne described Ella as "an extraordinary woman [who] had the gift of making life colourful."[2] She was a valued and respected friend to many in Dublin during those exciting and important years of the Celtic Revival. She shared ideas on mysticism, literature, and nationalism with AE (George Russell), William Butler Yeats, Padraic Colum, Standish O'Grady, Austin Clarke, and others who worked to preserve Irish culture. Yet her work was not all about lofty ideals. After the 1916 uprising (which she witnessed) she hid ammunition in her home for the Republican Army and when the treaty with England was signed that divided the sacred island of Eire, Ella Young's heart broke for she knew the magic had fled her native land.

In 1925 Ella Young came to America and took with her all the myths and legends and she wrote them down as stories and as poems and she lectured in town halls and great universities. Her audiences were enthralled – not only by Ella's great knowledge but also by the beauty and romance of her words. She became an important literary and spiritual figure in California, much as she had been in Dublin, influencing people like poet Robinson Jeffers, photographer Ansel Adams, artist John O'Shea, and composer Harry Partch. She found her faeries again in the sacred land of Point Lobos and in the isolation of her cottage garden near the dunes of Arroyo Grande.

In his 1922 book *Ireland's Literary Renaissance*, Ernest Boyd explains how AE brought to prominence "poets of the younger generation" who "had gathered about him" as part of Dublin's Theosophical movement. Ella Young was one of the poets AE chose for inclusion in his book *New Songs* (1904).[3] This prominent anthology launched Ella's reputation as an important contributor to the Irish literary scene of the early 20th century and her first monograph was released in 1906, simply entitled *Poems*. In this collection, Ella begins to explore the ancient myths of Ireland as represented in the poem "Finovar." This was a theme she continued throughout her life, both with her prose and her poetry, and was her great gift to Irish culture. From 1906 to 1950 she published seven books of poetry, five books of Irish tales, and her autobiography in 1945.

Ella's writing is rich in romanticism. As with her predecessors the Pre-Raphaelites, Ella drew her inspiration from nature and from the ancient tales. With her lyrical voice she painted images as vivid and dramatic as Holman Hunt and Dante Gabriel Rossetti placed upon canvas. Yet her literary style grew – becoming more concise, her words more economical. A beautiful example of her later work is "Artemis" (1950). In this poem Ella retains her mythical content yet in a form highly reminiscent of Haiku.

The moon took off her mask for me
Yester-night,
I saw her strange face
Ivory-white.

Crouching in the jungle, too,
The leopard saw:
And stretched in haughty greeting
A scimitar claw.

Later in life, Ella reveals some of her philosophy on writing in a letter to an aspiring poet:

"It is out of a strenuous rich life, out of dream, out of struggle, out of a fine perception of beauty that one writes... Try always for music and rhythm – just as thought and emotion are the soul, these things are the beautiful body of poetry."[4]

Her use of Celtic myth and legends, as well as Arthurian literature and faery lore, is considerable. Throughout an array of magical tales in such volumes as *The Wonder Smith and his Son* (1927) and *The Unicorn With Silver Shoes* (1932) she used her skilful poetic prose style to evoke a misty wonderland of magic and romance. Faery beings, drawn from her childhood memories of tales told to her by her mother and grandmother, later augmented by her wide reading and conversations with literary luminaries such as W.B. Yeats and George Russell (AE), dominate these collections, especially *The Coming of Lugh* (1909) and *Celtic Wonder Tales* (1910).

Most of these stories were written in her new home, America, where she seemed to see even more clearly the spiritual vision of her native land. As her friend of later life Jane Thompson reported: "To Ella [Young] the material world was no more real than the spirit world … the veil between them for her was very thin."

In *The Wonder Smith and His Son* she wrote:

"The pallor of dawn was in the air when a shriek tore the sleep from him. He sat up: great wings beat the sky making darkness above him, and something dropped to the earth within hand-reach. He fingered it – a bag of tools! As he touched them he knew he had the skill to use them though his hands had never hardened under a tool in his life. He slung his wallet over his shoulder and set off towards town."

Ella Young had her own skills and words were her tools. With them she drew pictures that remain in the mind long after one has finished reading them. She was, in every sense, a true Filid; her understanding of the magical worlds of the Celts, of the folk-lore and myths in which their ancient beliefs were preserved, shines out of everything she wrote. Few writers of this or any time have so perfectly captured the subtle nuances of style in which Celtic literature was written. Yeats had this ability, as did William Sharp (Fiona Macleod), but Ella Young surpasses them all when it comes to the poetic understanding of the ancient tales and the ethic which bound them.

In this collection we have striven to give as full a selection as possible from the writings of this remarkable woman – the faery tales, the delicate poetry, and the visionary gifts she brought to them all. Her use of Irish names and words was very idiosyncratic – as was her spelling. She used a number of Anglicised spellings of Irish names – for example *Gubbaun* for *Gobaun*. She also used a number of archaic words that enhance the overall romanticism of her work. We have preserved the original printed versions of names and unusual words to maintain the distinctive style of her work.

Ella Young deserves to be better known today; we hope that a new generation of readers will find things here they will come to love as much as we have.

Denise Sallee and John Matthews, 2010

1   Williams, J.E. Caerwyn and Patrick K. Ford. *The Irish Literary Tradition.* Cardiff, University of Wales Press, 1992. pp.23-25.
2   Jeffares, A. Norman and Anna McBride White, eds. *The Autobiography of Maud Gonne: A Servant of the Queen.* Chicago: University of Chicago Press, 1995. p.335.
3   Boyd, Ernest. *Ireland's Literary Renaissance.* New York: Alfred a. Knopf, 1916, 1922.
4   Ella Young to Ansel Adams, Los Gatos, California, n.d. Ansel Adams Archive, Center for Creative Photography, University of Arizona, Tucson, Arizona.

PART ONE:

STORIES AND POEMS

THE UNICORN WITH SILVER SHOES

(1932)

In this collection of stories, Ella Young turned naturally to her first love – Celtic myth and folklore. She says of the collection that it was "frankly a book for children, but since people always like what is not intended for them, perhaps a few grown-ups will read it also." She goes on to relate that these were stories she used to tell to children who "had a fondness for tales about Ogres, Magicians and Strange Beasts." These we find a-plenty in this sparkling collection, which introduces us to Ballor's Son, a kind of wild trickster figure with an insatiable curiosity about everything, who seems to owe a good deal to the British Puck (who also appears in his Irish guise as the Pooka) as well as to traditional Irish heroes such a Fionn mac Cumhail or the Amadan Mor (Great Fool). A huge panoply of Irish gods and goddesses also appear in these stories. As in all of Ella Young's tales the presence of such beings is seen as a perfectly natural state of affairs, and she puts contemporary language into their mouths alongside the 'high speech' of epic. Above all, these tales are threaded though with Ella Young's passion for magic and the power of the ancient Irish legends she knew and loved so well.

THREE GOLDEN APPLES

Ballor's Son woke in the morning with a grievance in his mind.

"What's the good of having a king for your father," he said to himself, "if you never get anything that you want? I wish I wasn't Ballor's only son. I wish I lived in a country where there was sunshine in the sky and apples on the trees – Oh, I wish I were a beggar-boy with the world to wander in!"

He felt so sorry for himself that he began to cry, softly at first and then loudly – very loudly indeed.

The First Lord-in-Waiting hurried in, with the Second Lord-in-Waiting at his heels.

"O Noble Prince," said the First Lord, "what distresses you?"

"I want an apple tree!" said Ballor's Son. "I want a white horse that can go over land and water; I want a silver branch with three golden apples on it!"

"Alas!" said the First Lord-in-Waiting, wiping a tear out of his eyes.

"Alas!" said the Second Lord, copying him.

"Alas!" said the two of them together. "You've been listening to Faery tales, Most Noble Prince!"

"I have not!" said Ballor's son, stoutly.

"Where did you get word, then," said the First Lord, "of a Horse that goes over land and sea, or of the Silver Branch with Golden Apples?"

"I got word of them from a boy I met in the Garden of Twisted Trees in the dusk of yestereve, the time I ran away from you all. He told me of those things – and other things too. Oh, I wish I had him to talk to now!"

"Don't wish a bad wish like that," said the First Lord, severely, "or you may find yourself in Faery-Land, for it was a lad out of Faery-Land that told you of the Golden Apples and of the White Horse. That Horse belongs to Mananaun the King of Faery-Land; and the Golden Apples belong to his son, Angus."

"And to what person does the Pooka belong?" said Ballor's Son.

"The Pooka," said the First Lord, "is a tricky little spirit that belongs to Faery-Land: and the less you trouble your head about these things the better!"

"How does one go to Faery-Land?" asked Ballor's Son.

"No one in this country knows," said the First Lord, "and of a certainty you, Most Noble Prince, are not going there!"

Ballor's Son shut his lips tightly; he had got as much information as he was likely to get, and he had made up his mind.

He was so very good all day that he was given his best royal crown to wear and his best royal mantle. He had both these on him when he stole away in the dusk to look for Faery-Land.

Beyond the Garden of Twisted Trees there was a high wall, and on top of the wall a row of sharp iron spikes. The sky was beyond the wall, and nothing else that Ballor's Son could see. He went from end to end of the wall, looking for a doorway, or a loose place in the stones where he could climb, or a broken place where he could crawl out, but he found everywhere the same solid smooth iron-spiked wall.

He sat down on the ground, and nothing but the thought of the First and Second Lords-in-Waiting prevented him from lifting his voice in a wail fitting to the occasion.

"I *won't* cry," he said to himself. "No, I won't cry – to please them!"

All at once he knew that he was not alone. Beside him stood the boy he had spoken with the evening before. He was a slender lad with pale gold hair and shining grey eyes.

"Put your hand in mine," he said to Ballor's Son, "and I will take you into Faery-Land."

Ballor's Son reached a hand. He heard a sound like a clap of thunder, and shut his eyes tight. When he opened them he was all by himself in a wood. He had never seen trees like the trees of that wood, so tall-growing, so ancient, so splendid-looking. On all the boughs the leaves were young and green and the sunlight flaming through them made patterns on the moss about his feet. A little path wound away and away into the heart of the wood. Ballor's Son went along the path. It seemed to him that he walked and walked and walked for hours before he came to an open space, and peering through the branches, saw an old man seated on a stone.

Ballor's Son thought that he must be very old, because his hair was grey to whiteness, but when he looked closer that hair was all like silver flame and the old man had a radiance in his face. He was wrapped in a cloak of purple that had nine capes, each one more richly embroidered than the other. By his side stood a young man with a sunburnt face and poor and tattered clothes. They were talking together. Ballor's Son sharpened his ears to listen.

"Are you not tired," asked the old man, "are you not tired, Angus, of walking the roads of the world with the bitter wind in your face and the clogging dust on your feet? Are you still eager to leave riches and go a-begging?"

"I am still eager," said the young man, "for change, though it be from blue to grey: and for the road where all things may happen!"

Just then, a Pooka came out from between the trees. It looked like a little snow-white kid with golden horns and silver hoofs, but it could take any shape it had a fancy for. When it saw Angus it smiled and made one jump on to his shoulder.

"Look at this!" said Angus, "I never can say anything important without being interrupted!"

"What do you want?" he said to the Pooka, pretending to be cross.

"Oh, nothing at all, only to listen to your wise talk; it does me good," said the Pooka, prancing on Angus' shoulder. "I'll soon be the wisest Pooka in the world!"

At this Ballor's Son burst out of hiding.

"Pooka! Pooka! Pooka!" he yelled, "I want you, come here!"

The Pooka jumped behind Angus. Ballor's Son tried to seize it. Angus put out his hand.

"Who are you?" he said.

"I am a Royal Prince," said the boy trying to look big.

"You have princely manners," said Angus.

"I am Ballor's own son. I have come out to look for treasure, and if you have anything, I command you to give it to me at once."

"What would you like?" said Angus.

"I would like the White Horse of Mananaun, or three Golden Apples, or a Hound out of Faery-Land."

"They say it's lucky to be good to poor folk," said Angus, "if you are good to us perhaps you may find a treasure."

"If you do not get up at once and hunt about for a treasure for me, I will tell my father, Ballor, and he will wither you off the face of the earth!"

"Oh, give me a little time," said Angus, "and I'll look for something."

The Pooka, who had been listening to everything, now skipped out from his hiding-place with a turnip in his mouth – he was holding it by the green leaves.

"The very thing!" said Angus. "Here is a treasure!" He took the turnip in his hands and passed his fingers over it. The turnip became a great white egg, and the leaves turned into gold and crimson spots and spread themselves over the egg.

"Now look at this!" said Angus. "It is an enchanted egg. You have only to keep it till you do three Good Actions, and then it will hatch out into something splendid."

"Will it hatch into Mananaun's White Horse?" asked Ballor's Son.

"It depends on the Good Actions you do: everything depends on that."

"What is Good Action?"

"Well, if you were to go quietly away, and never tell anyone you had seen us, it would be a Good Action."

"I'll go," said Ballor's Son. He took the egg in his hands, kicked up a toe-full of earth at the Pooka, and went.

He hadn't gone far when he heard a bird singing. He looked and saw a little bird on a furze bush.

"Stop that noise!" he said.

The bird kept on singing. Ballor's Son flung the egg at it. The egg turned into a turnip, and struck a hare that was couching in the ferns by the furze bush.

"My curse on you!" cried Ballor's Son, "for a brittle egg! What came over you to hatch into nothing better than a hare! My Grief and my Trouble! What came over you to hatch out at all when this is only my second Good Action?"

He turned to go back to his own country. At first he walked with big steps puffing his cheeks vaingloriously, but little by little a sense of loss overcame him and as he thought how nearly he had earned the White Horse of Mananaun, or three Golden apples, or some greater treasure, two tears slowly rolled down his snub nose.

Angus and the old man and the Pooka were still in the little clearing when Ballor's Son passed back through it. The moment he came in sight, the Pooka changed himself into a squirrel and ran up the oak tree; Angus changed himself into an oak leaf and fell softly on a bank of moss; the old man sat quite still and looked at Ballor's Son.

"The egg hatched out," said Ballor's Son. "It was a bad egg, I wish that I had thrown it at the beggar-man's head!"

The old man smiled and picked up the oak leaf. He pressed his hands over it and it became a great golden egg with green and purple spots on it.

"Give it to me! Give it to me!" yelled Ballor's Son, "it's better than the first egg, and the first egg is broken. Give it to me."

"This egg is too precious for you," said the old man. "I must keep it in my own hands."

"Then I will blast you and all the forest and every living thing! I have only to roar three times, and three armies of my people will come to help me. Give me the egg, or I will roar."

"I will keep this egg in my own hands," said the old man.

Ballor's Son shut his eyes tight and opened his mouth wide to let out a great roar, and it is likely he would have been heard at the other end of the world if the Pooka hadn't dropped a handful of acorns into his mouth. The roar never came out. Ballor's Son choked and sputtered. The old man patted him on the back and shook him. He shook him very hard, and after a while Ballor's Son got his breath: then he said:

"I will not blast you this time; I will do a Good Action. I will let you carry the egg, and you can be my slave and treasure-finder!"

"I am Mananaun," said the old man.

"Oh," cried Ballor's Son, "O, I want a white – "

He heard the Pooka laughing behind him.

"What are you laughing at?" he cried, turning sharply round.

There was no Pooka! There was no laughter! He turned again. There was no old man, and no bank of moss!

He rubbed his eyes, he shut them and opened them three times, he dug his knuckles into them – there was no Pooka, no bank of moss, no old man!

"What ails you, Ballor's Son?" said a voice. It came from a tree above him, and looking up he saw a white bird with a ruby-coloured breast and emerald eyes.

"I'm the most unfortunate prince that ever lived!" said Ballor's Son. "I've lost my Luck-Egg."

"I've lost three Seeds of Good-Luck, myself," said the bird.

"What are Seeds of Good-Luck?" asked Ballor's Son. "Are they as good as Luck-Eggs?"

"That depends," said the bird, "on the person who plants them – they might grow into anything!"

"Where did you lose them?" asked Ballor's Son.

"In the hollow of the tree I'm sitting on," said the bird.

"I'll get them," said Ballor's Son, and he began to break his way into the hollow of the tree. It was hard work, but he kept at it till he could put head and shoulder and a searching hand into the hollow. He found three hard, shining seeds. Straightening himself he cried:

"I've got them, White Bird."

The bird had gone.

"I'll keep them myself," said Ballor's Son.

"Will you?" asked a voice with laughter in it – a voice that he knew.

It was the Pooka come back!

This time he looked like a great stag with branching horns. His hide was silver spotted with gold.

"Give the seeds to me," he said, "and I will let you ride on my back."

"No," cried Ballor's Son, "I will give the seeds to the owner!"

"That will be a Good Action," said the Pooka.

"White Bird! White Bird! White Bird!" cried Ballor's Son.

From the far blueness of the sky the white bird descended, whirling and poising and falling as lightly as a petal of apple-blossom or a flake of wind-lifted snow.

"Give the seeds to Angus, the Beggar-Man, with my blessing," cried the white bird, circling and poising.

"Angus! Angus! Angus!" cried Ballor's Son, and before the last word left his mouth the beggar-man was standing between the trees.

Ballor's Son gave him the seeds.

Angus took the seeds. He put one on his forehead where it shone like a king's jewel. He threw one into the air and it became a golden bird, circling and poising with its ruby-breasted fellow. He planted one. It came up a little slender apple tree. It grew and blossomed, and three big yellow apples hung on it – the sweetest apples in all the world! Angus gathered the apples. He kept one. He gave one to the Pooka.

"Good luck, and may your hand never be empty," said the Pooka.

He gave one to Ballor's Son.

"Here," said he, "is fruit untasted save in Faery-Land. Keep it till you go into your own country, or no one will believe you ever had it."

"Good luck, and may your hand never be empty," said Ballor's Son. He stepped blithely homeward, but he hadn't taken three steps before he fell to munching the apple – that is why no one believed him when he got home.

KYELINS, BLUE AND GREEN

Ballor's Son sat with Flame of Joy in the Wood of Pomegranates. It was noonday and very still except when a small wind stole through the branches to listen to what Flame of Joy and Ballor's Son were saying to each other.

"I think," said Flame of Joy, "that you should take exercise, that's the thing you ought to have."

"I always eat all my food," said Ballor's Son. "The First Lord says it is my duty to the kingdom."

"I'm not speaking about food. You eat too much. What you need is something to thin you down and keep you slender, you ought to run and leap and turn rainbow-somersaults."

"I don't know how to," said Ballor's Son.

"Well, there isn't a rainbow anywhere about or I'd show you. See that slanting sunbeam. It's just the right kind to run up. Keep your eyes on me!"

There was indeed a sunbeam slanting between two pomegranate boughs. Flame of Joy leaped lightly on it and ran up it between the boughs. Soon he was out of sight. Ballor's Son wondered if he would keep on running till he lost himself in the sky, but quite suddenly he slid down a beam that slanted under two boughs, and threw himself on the moss beside Ballor's Son.

"Good exercise!" he said.

"I won't run up a sunbeam," said Ballor's Son.

"Well, you might begin with something easier. You might try to run as the wind does, just a little above the earth. Like this."

Flame of Joy took a deep breath and leaped free of the ground, then he ran over the moss tufts and the lily cups all starry and slender without touching them.

It was a delight of the heart to look at him, and Ballor's Son gave a joy-shout. Flame of Joy running lightly past him reached down a hand:

"Come," he said, "draw a deep breath and run with me!"

Ballor's Son took a deep breath and a firm grip on Flame of Joy's hand and found himself running lightly over the lily-heads without touching them until such a time as Flame of Joy bounced suddenly down on a mossy cushion, and drew Ballor's Son beside him.

"Not bad for a first attempt," he said. "What you need is practice, I would teach you quite a lot of things if you practiced hard enough."

"I don't mind if I run again," said Ballor's Son. "Give me your hand."

"No, you must try it now by yourself. Take a big breath and leap."

Ballor's Son took a deep breath and leaped free of the ground. He ran a few paces and was just going to cry, "Look at me," when he suddenly fell full length and bumped his forehead. Stifling a yell, for he remembered that on such occasions the first Lord always said, "Be dignified," he sat up sullenly and said:

"I have had enough exercise for today."

"That much exercise," said Flame of Joy, "is not worth talking of. I have a ploy in mind. We'll go into the country, catch a couple of Kyelins and ride them. I daresay you could stick on a Kyelin."

"Kyelins are not ridden," said Ballor's Son. "They are Sacred Beasts. Kyelins would bite large pieces out of us."

"Not if we were invisible," said Flame of Joy, "and had the courage to bridle them. I know where to get two Cloaks of Invisibility. I'll borrow them, and we'll hunt up the Kyelins."

"You can bridle Kyelins if you want to," said Ballor's Son. "I don't want to ride a Kyelin."

"Oh, yes, you will when I give you a Cloak," said Flame of Joy, "just lean against a tree and count leaf-shadows on the moss till I come back."

Flame of Joy was scarcely gone till he was back. He carried two cloaks fine as cobwebs and glittering with every colour of day and night. He put one on himself, wrapped the other round Ballor's Son, and said:

"Now reach your hand to me, shut your eyes, think steadily of those Kyelins, and I'll take you wind-running."

Ballor's Son reached a hand, shut his eyes and felt himself running, or rather floating, light as a wind-borne leaf. Presently he was aware of a many-throated murmur and a stir of people below him. Flame of Joy gripped him tighter, jerked him slightly, and said:

"Here we are."

Ballor's Son opened his eyes. Flame of Joy looked gorgeous in that Cloak, and Ballor's Son surveying himself was aware that he looked gorgeous also. But it was plain that they were invisible. Ballor's Son was sorry at first that they were invisible, with so many eager eyes about. They were in the great plaza of Ballor's City. Ballor's palanquin was there with lords and slaves about it: everywhere in the great plaza were lords and warriors of the Fomor. Magicians were leading out a procession of Sacred Animals to honour the Cat of Cruachan. Very great and much to be honoured and reverenced indeed was the Cat of Cruachan. His Temple of jacinth and chalcedony filled one whole side of the plaza, flaunting the pallid sky. Domed it was and turreted multitudinously: every turret of hammered silver inset with malachite, every dome of red gold.

Leashed in chains and collars of gold and led by black slant-eyed magicians, the beasts passed: Marocots, bulky and slow-moving, with ears that swept the ground; double-headed Llanitos, white as snow; Gryphons; fire-breathing Dragons; scaled Chimæras; Kyelins walking two and two, a blue Kyelin beside a green Kyelin. Midmost of the plaza, making a gorgeousness about it, was Ballor's palanquin crusted with gems and gold. Ballor sat there, blind – for he dared not open the one terrible eye that he had in the centre of his forehead. That eye was the ruin of cities and the devastation of armies. It killed more swiftly than a lightning stroke. Ballor sat in his palanquin – blind – and the beasts were led before him two by two. He stretched his hands over them and said:

"My benison to you: strength and pride and length of days. Make glad, make glad the festival of the Cat of Cruachan!"

"Ballor's Son," said Flame of Joy, "do you see those two Kyelins with gilded tails and tusks and black manes that are coming up now? We will ride those Kyelins. When they come a-breast of us, be ready! You take the green Kyelin. I'll catch the blue one."

"Look at their claws," said Ballor's Son. "Look at their teeth! They will just make one bite of us!"

"No they won't," said Flame of Joy. "I have got something that I did not tell you about. I brought a hazel rod for each of us out of the Hazel Wood that is near the Garden of Delight that Angus has. If we strike the Kyelins with those rods they will be tame."

"I'll strike my Kyelin at the beginning," said Ballor's Son.

"If you do, you'll lose a lot of fun," said Flame of Joy.

"I'll have fun enough watching your Kyelin," said Ballor's Son.

By this the Kyelins were well a-breast. Ballor's Son reached out and struck the green Kyelin with his hazel rod. The beast stood stock-still, so astonished was he, and Ballor's Son climbed carefully on his back, gripped his black mane, and began to swathe his head and eyes in a fold of the Cloak. Flame of Joy thrust the hazel rod in his girdle and leaped on the back of the blue Kyelin.

With a scream the beast stood upright. His scythed paws tore the air, he leaped and writhed as though he had sustained a mortal hurt.

"Strike him with the rod," said Ballor's Son.

"No," cried Flame of Joy. "I am going to bridle him," and bridle him he did, with a fold of the Cloak thrust between his gaping jaws.

Round and round in maddened dizzying circles swung the blue Kyelin, screaming and striking at everybody and everything. His priest-custodians dropped the golden chains and ran. Everywhere people shouted and ran. The crowded plaza swayed like a sea-wave that topples over on itself.

Llanitos and Gryphons broke loose, tearing and clawing. Marocots trampled and trumpeted, Chimæras writhed and struck. And all the while the blue Kyelin screamed and gyrated, till of a sudden the fold of Cloak that bridled him slipped from his screeching mouth and completely covered his face and head. Rage held him motionless and dumb. The folk nearest him had time to rally.

"The Kyelin is headless!" they cried. "The Sacred Kyelins are headless both, yet they live! Sorcerers have done this! Sorcerers and warlocks are amongst us! Those that walk invisible are come to destroy us! We are stricken! We are doomed. Destruction is come to the City of Ballor!"

"Let Ballor open his Eye and smite his enemies!" cried some.

"No, no," shrieked others. "That is the worst destruction, the consuming fire! We are but ashes and fire dust before the Eye of Ballor. Call on the Cat of Cruachan, let him succour us, the Mighty One!"

"Call on the Cat of Cruachan, invoke the Cat of Cruachan," cried voices everywhere. "Prostrate yourselves. Rend your garments. Call on the Cat of Cruachan!"

A gong sounded above the crying of men and beasts, smiting the confusion and tumult.

Boum – Boum – Boum – Boum –

The Arch-Priest was striking it in the Temple of the Cat. At the sound of that gong priests everywhere lifted their voices in a chant:

"O Mighty Cat of Cruachan
Hear us
Succour us
Protect us
Protect the Sacred Beasts
Hear us, Cat of Cruachan!"

"Hear us!" cried the people. "Hear us, Cat of Cruachan! Succour us! Protect us! Hear us! Hear us! Hear us!"

Boum – Boum – Boum – Boum –

Suddenly the air trembled. The sky bulged and shook like a tent-flap. There was a roar that loosened the very roots of the hills: and out of that roar, out of nothingness the Cat of Cruachan flashed into being. He was immense. The brightness of him was terrible. He glittered amongst the broken standards and overturned palanquins with a blinding magnificence.

"The Cat of Cruachan! The Cat of Cruachan!" cried the people, throwing themselves on their faces.

"We are lost!" whispered Flame of Joy, crouching low on his Kyelin. "The Cat of Cruachan can see us! He belongs to the world of Faery!"

Ballor's Son huddled further into his Cloak, and crouched low as Flame of Joy was crouching.

Meteor-swift the Cat approached. With a turn of the head he flung Flame of Joy across his shoulders. A second turn, and Ballor's Son was on his shoulders too!

Then he stretched his mighty flanks and bounded into the air in a great arching leap. That leap took him over the arid sabre-sharp mountains and poisonous waters that encircle Ballor's Country.

A second time he stretched his mighty flanks and bounded into the air in a great arching leap. That leap took him over Harmotrasan, the mountain of black obsidian that shuts out half the world and draws to itself the dark light of the moon.

A third time he stretched his mighty flanks and bounded into the air in a great arching leap. That leap took him over Gormidon, the mountain of chalcedony that blossoms against the stars and draws to itself the bright light of the moon.

A fourth leap that he made took him over Frondisande, the mountain of the Silver Unicorns, where the moon walks with lingering footsteps, where she loiters on nights that she does not show herself in the sky.

When the Cat had crossed that mountain he was in Cruachan, his own country. He widened his padded feet joyously and dug his sickle-sharp claws into the earth, the way a cat does – a caress to his own country. Then he lowered his great head, and Flame of Joy and Ballor's Son came foot to ground falling with clutched hands in a huddled shame-faced heap.

"It is small and innocent ye look," said the Cat, "to have stirred up such a turmoil."

"I wish the ground would open," said Ballor's Son, "and swallow up every Kyelin in the world: I wish it would!"

"You have affronted the Sacred Beasts," said the Cat, "and they are under my protection. It is a cause of offence."

"I wish I hadn't 'fronted them," said Ballor's Son, "I wish I'd never been born. I do!"

"I made him ride the Kyelin," said Flame of Joy. "He didn't want to. It was a ploy that I thought of."

"Oh, it was a ploy of yours, and you are one who runs foot to foot with the Pooka in the Country of the Ever-Young. What brought you a-mischief making into the Land of the Fomor? What made you think of that ploy?"

"We needed exercise."

The cat considered Flame of Joy with grave attention for a few moments. Then he said:

"At times I need exercise myself. You have my permission, you and Ballor's Son, to find your own way home from Cruachan. It will be exercise, good and plentiful."

Flame of Joy flung himself forehead to the earth and cried out:

"O Jewel of Two Worlds, O Mighty Lord beloved of the Sun, O Splendour of the Forest, O darling of every star in heaven, do not destroy us! We could not live and cross the mountain of the Silver Unicorns."

"Have you it in mind that you could cross Harmotrasan and Gormidon?" asked the Cat.

"I have it in mind that we could try."

"Oh, no," sobbed Ballor's Son, who had also prostrated himself forehead to earth. "Oh, no, we could not try. Great Cat of Cruachan, we could not cross the mountains. Oh, I want to go home!"

"Which of you two," said the Cat, "has the greater spark of intelligence?"

Ballor's Son sat up and stared at the Cat of Cruachan. So did Flame of Joy.

"What's intelligence?" asked Ballor's Son.

"If you were not here," said the Cat, "where would you be?"

"At home," said Ballor's Son.

"I am not so sure of that," said the Cat. "You might be trampled out of semblance to yourself by the crowd in the plaza, or clawed to pieces by a Kyelin, or tossed half-way to the moon by one of the horned Chimæras!"

"Try *me* with a question," said Flame of Joy.

"I will," said the Cat, "*what is that you find without seeking, seek without finding, and carry about with you because you cannot be rid of it?*"

"Let me think," said Flame of Joy.

"I know," said Ballor's Son, "it's a riddle like what First Lord asks when I'm lonesome in the evenings. There is only one true answer to a riddle!"

"It is a riddle," said the Cat, "and if one or other of you answer it, I will take you across the mountain of the Silver Unicorns."

"*What is it that one finds without seeking?*" repeated Flame of Joy, clasping his head with his hands and rocking to and fro as he sat, "what is it one finds – Perhaps it is Pooka, one always meets him where no one would expect him."

"It is not the Pooka," said the Cat.

"Maybe it is the wind," said Flame of Joy.

"It is not the wind," said the Cat.

"I have it," shouted Ballor's Son. "I know the answer. It's like a riddle the First Lord gave me once:

> "*He went to the wood and got it*
> *He sat him down and sought it*
> *And because he could not find it*
> *He brought it home with him.*"

"I know the answer to that riddle. The one true answer:

"A thorn in the foot!"

"Luck favours you," said the Cat. "The first Lord may chance to lay eyes on you again. You have answered my riddle. Climb both of you on my shoulders, take a good grip, and we will set out."

They did not need to be told a second time. Joyfully they climbed those mischance-defying shoulders.

"Hold tight now," said the Cat, and with one splendid bound he rose in the air, cleared the mountain of the Unicorns and landed on the topmost ridge of the mountain of chalcedony.

There seemed to be miles of that mountain as Flame of Joy and Ballor's Son surveyed it from the Cat's shoulders: meadows of it, amethyst and agate-grey and silvery blue; crevasses of it, violet-dark; and crags of it, flung up like wave-crests, milky crystal.

"What plan commends itself to you," said the Cat, "for the crossing of this mountain?"

"I can wind-run," said Flame of Joy, "and so can Ballor's Son when I hold his hand. We will wind-run till we come to an end of the mountain."

"It is a long way to the end of it," said the Cat, "but wind-running is good exercise. Stand on my back and take-off."

They climbed to their feet in the space between his broad shoulders.

"We thank you, noble Cat of Cruachan, Jewel of Two Worlds," said Flame of Joy, "for the help that you have given to us. May your shadow – golden in one World, ebony in the other – never grow less!"

"May the wind bear you lightly," said the Cat of Cruachan.

"Now," said Flame of Joy, "reach me your hand. Draw a deep breath. Shut your eyes – and we start!"

Ballor's Son took a firm grip of the hand that Flame of Joy stretched out to him, drew a deep breath, shut his eyes, and they leaped clear of the Cat's shoulders.

They were wind-running. They were wind-running, on the mountain of chalcedony!

Swiftly they ran – swiftly, swiftly, swiftly, and more swiftly still.

It was good wind-running. Flame of Joy stretched himself in his stride, and Ballor's Son put strength and heart into it.

Good wind-runners they! Swift and swifter yet. Wind-running on the mountain of chalcedony!

It seemed to Ballor's Son that hours – and days – and years spent themselves in that running. At first he was proud to be vaunting. He joyed in the lightness of his body and in his sturdiness of will. He joyed in the adventure. But too many hours and years went by! He thought of supper-time and the lighted candles. He thought of his bed that had soft pillows in it and warm coverlets. He thought of the First Lord, angry and flustered: it was cheering to think of the First Lord. He thought of Eblis the great Djinn that was a friend of his and took him for joy-flights sitting between his outspread wings. When he thought of Eblis, tears trickled between his eyelids and ran one after another down his cheek.

In a while he could not keep his eyes shut any longer. He snatched a look. Beneath him the mountain of chalcedony flowed endlessly: like a stream, like a torrent, like a cataract, like a sea. Its ridged crevasses were wave-crests; its canyons wave-hollows; the white and purple of it a many-patterned sliding sea-floor! Terror gripped Ballor's Son. His heart twisted within him.

"I am falling," he cried, "the mountain is sucking me down. O Flame of Joy, hold me, hold fast to me!"

Flame of Joy held fast, and they came down together. It was a hard bump, but they had no chance to finger their bruises. In the place where they fell, the mountain-slant was smooth as polished ice. They slid, and slid, and slid – and slid, holding to each other. At length a blue jut of rock halted them. When they came to themselves they struggled to their feet:

"We must wind-run again," said Flame of Joy, "and at once! Hold fast to me, take a deep breath and leap clear!"

"I can't take a deep breath – I can't – I can't!" sobbed Ballor's Son. "It hurts me to breathe. My legs hurt me. Oh, I'm losing foothold – I'm falling. I'm falling again!"

"Put some heart into you!" cried Flame of Joy. "You're on your feet as it is. You can leap clear if you make trial of it. Know, draw a deep breath – and put lightness into your body!"

Ballor's Son laboured to draw a deep breath, but try as he might he could not leap clear. He could not give lightness to his body – he could not wind-run!

"My grief!" said Flame of Joy. "That ever the thought of a Kyelin crossed my mind! We are like to end our days on this mountain."

"O Flame of Joy," cried Ballor's Son, "do not leave me. You can wind-run, but do not leave me – do not leave me!"

"Who spoke of leaving you?" said Flame of Joy. "Have sense, and make some kind of a quietness. I'm trying to work out in my head how long it will take us to walk."

He cast a resentful look about him. On all sides the mountain enpeaked and encompassed them. There was nothing but mountain and sky – sky and mountain! They were in a country of translucent stone; milky amethyst and azure in the sunlight, purpled in the shadow to violet and the hue of the wild iris. It had neither twig nor grass-blade, but here and there the wide stone reaches of it seemed to be frosted with blossoms.

"We might get a barefoot grip," said Flame of Joy, "unthong your shoes!"

Ballor's Son huddled himself in a crotch of the rock-jut, and with clumsy and unaccustomed fingers began to unloose his richly furred and embroidered shoes.

"What will we do," he asked, "when we come to a place with sharp stones that cut our feet?"

"It is a chance that we must take with the other chances. We have no choice."

"Flame of Joy," said Ballor's Son, halting from his labours. "You can wind-run."

"What's the good of it, when you can't?"

"You could go to your own country. You could find Angus and come back for me. I could stay in the shelter of this rock till you came."

"No one is sure of finding Angus," said Flame of Joy, "he wanders at his will in all the worlds. And how could I find you again in the bleached wastes and vastnesses of this mountain?"

Ballor's Son threw back his head and sobbed with resolution and vigour.

"I can't walk," he sobbed, "it's all as smooth as glass everywhere away from this rock!"

"I'll go first and you can hold to me. We have no time to lose. Now!"

Ballor's Son, palanquined and slave-attended, was little used to walking. He found it hard to balance himself on his bare feet, and stumbling almost at the first step he clutched Flame of Joy. Flame of Joy tottered, and only by the litheness of his body recovered himself.

"Have a care," he said, "or we'll find ourselves crawling down this slope on our hands and knees."

It was indeed how they found themselves a few moments later, only they were not crawling. They were sliding – fast, and faster, and faster yet!

It was not a rock-jut that halted them this time. It was something warm and soft and furry. It was the great padded foot of the Cat of Cruachan!

Pure gold against the crystal and amethyst of the mountain, the Cat sprawled at full length on the crevassed slope. His scimitar-sharp claws, translucent as agate, were curved idly in a nonchalant claw-caress. Between his claws Ballor's Son and Flame of Joy were buttressed.

"*What is it,*" said the Cat, "*that goes with equal swiftness over land and sea, carries no rider, and leaves no mark of its running?*"

"The White Horse of Mananaun," said Ballor's Son promptly.

"The Horse of Mananaun carries a rider," said the Cat.

"Maybe it's the wind," said Ballor's Son.

"It's not the wind," said the Cat.

"I know what it is," said Flame of Joy, "a thing that I have not seen often, sliding from hillside to lake. *It is the shadow of a cloud.*"

"Your eyes have served you well," said the Cat, "you have answered my riddle. I will take you over the mountain Harmotrasan and beyond it, for I will set you down within a stone's throw of the Wood of Pomegranates. Climb on my shoulders."

They climbed and took a joyous neck-grip.

The Cat walked with leisurely steps to where a long crevasse sank from violet-blue to an abysmal blackness. On the crevasse-edge he balanced himself for a spring, and with a sinewy space-devouring leap launched his bulk against the sky.

When his feet touched earth he was on the verge of the Wood of Pomegranates. The sun slanted low among the ruby-coloured fruits. It was late afternoon.

Gently he lowered Ballor's Son and Flame of Joy from his shoulders. Speechless they were because of their delight in the swift motion and in the homecoming.

"My benison on both of you," said the Cat of Cruachan. "Do not harass the Sacred Beasts. Do not disregard the advice of your elders. Be good and you will be happy. Farewell."

In a flash he was gone.

"I wish he hadn't hurried off like that," said Flame of Joy. "I was thinking out a farewell wish to say to him."

"Keep it in your mind," said Ballor's Son, "and we can say it to the Pooka some time when he is going away in a huff."

"You have no sense of the fitness of things," said Flame of Joy, "epithets that would suit the Cat of Cruachan would seem to deride the Pooka."

"What are epithets?" said Ballor's Son.

"If you ask me another question, Ballor's Son, I'll just stretch out on the grass and die! You'd better think of what you are going to say to the First Lord and the Second Lord and all your household when you get back to the Palace."

"I won't say anything," said Ballor's Son. "I never say anything when I come back from being with you. They don't ask me now where I was. It makes me sulky. The First Lord is careful not to anger me – it is bad for my constitution! He told the Second Lord that I must have found a hiding place in the Pleasaunce, and it was best to humour me about it."

"But the Kyelins and the Plaza," said Flame of Joy, "won't they ask about that?"

"I kept inside my Cloak of Invisibility; you had your Cloak."

"How wise you are," said Flame of Joy, "I never thought of the Cloaks, and we still have them wrapped about us! I might have forgotten to take back the one you have. Give it to me. Now – Mum's the word!"

"Mum's the word," said Ballor's Son resolutely, as he turned toward the magic gap that he knew of in the wall of Ballor's Pleasaunce.

THE UNICORN WITH SILVER SHOES

Ballor's Son was thinking hard: a deep line showed between his eyebrows, his nose was screwed to a point of attention, and with both hands he clutched the straight locks that fell on either side of his face, as if to hold his head on the anchorage of his shoulders. With the stress of thinking, the hair on top of his head rose in a point.

"I won't bear it any longer," he said out loud. "I'll run away."

He got to his feet and stamped resolutely.

"Yes," he said, "I'll run away: that's what I'll do."

"Did you call, Illustrious One?" said the First Lord-in-Waiting, entering the room.

"No!" said Ballor's Son, "I did not call, I don't want to see you, or the Second Lord-in-Waiting either, but since you can't keep to yourself you may as well tell me what I could do all day long if I were not King Ballor's only son. What could happen if I were the son of the Keeper of the Kyelins with Tufted Ears?"

"You could learn to do something useful," said the First Lord-in-Waiting, "you would have to work for your living. You would have to think twice before you spoke once."

"I was thinking once," said the prince, "when you interrupted me: I am going into the garden now to think twice without interruptions.

Don't come near me till I send for you, or till it is time for me to look at the Parade of Green Dragons."

He held his head up and walked as he had seen his father walk when he told his Councillors that they were fools: and he walked in that fashion down the marble steps from his balcony and down the flagged path in the garden till he came to the blank wall that shut the sky out at the end of Ballor's pleasaunce.

Ballor's Son looked very small and helpless in the shadow of that wall, but he did not feel helpless. He struck his hands together and cried:

"Come Playfellow Mine,
Come Flame of Joy,
Come from the Apple Wood
Come from between the Silver Oaks
Come from between the boughs of the Pomegranate Trees:
Come, come, Playfellow Mine!"

When Ballor's Son had said this in a loud voice he said it over again very softly: then he shut his eyes tight and said it a third time. When he opened his eyes he was beyond the wall. He was under the boughs of the pomegranate trees. Those boughs were very old and twisted and wrinkled: where the light struck them they were silver-coloured and the leaves were like leaves of jade. The pomegranates were so large that they looked like ruby lanthorns. Standing close to Ballor's Son was a lad about his own age, a slender youth in a gold tunic.

"I have a secret to tell you, Flame of Joy," said Ballor's Son. "I'm going to run away from everybody and everything and stay in your country always."

"But the people of the Land of the Ever-Young belong to it," said Flame of Joy, "and you would never have been here at all if I had not brought you."

"I mean to earn my living in the Land of the Ever-Young," said Ballor's Son, "and I want you to give me some Good Advice."

"We had better ask Angus for Good Advice," said Flame of Joy, "come, let us find him."

They went through the Wood of Pomegranates and then through the Wood of the Silver Oaks till they came to the Wood of Apple Trees and there under a blossomed tree they saw Angus the Ever-Young. He was sitting with his back against the tree and he was as bright to look at as a garden of flowers, for he had a robe embroidered in every colour and his hair was wound about a gold disc on either side of his head. He had a small stringed instrument of music in his hands and drawing a sound now and again from it. The Pooka sat at a little distance regarding him gravely. Today the Pooka, who could take any shape, had made himself look like a white cat with golden spots. He had very long black tufts on his ears and a black tuft on his tail and his gold-taloned paws were black underneath.

"Now listen," Angus was saying, as the two boys came along, "this is how the song goes:

> *"My love is like a reed that sways*
> *Sings and sways*
> *By the side of the river:*
> *I am a fool to trust what she says*
> *Now – or ever.*
>
> *So light she is, so white she is,*
> *So bright, so dear:*
> *I'd fling the sun and moon away*
> *If she were here.*
>
> *O if she had a stead fast heart*
> *What man can say!*
> *I might be then too wise myself*
> *To fling the sun away."*

"If the song had been about me," said the Pooka, "I might have praised it, for one should encourage poets – as it is, however…"

"What!" said Angus.

"The song has many faults," said the Pooka, "I could make a better one myself:

> *"When I see you blink your eyes*
> *I think how wise*
> *A poet is:*
> *But your words shake me*
> *Your words make me*
> > *Rise*
> *And walk away:*
> *They make me say*
> *"Alack-a-Day!"*

"Does not this strike you as a most admirable elegy, Ballor's Son?" said the Pooka, turning sharply around.

"I see no sense in it," said Ballor's Son.

"If you did," said the Pooka, "the whole point of my little poem would be lost."

"Pooka," said Angus, "have I not begged you many times to suit your conversation to your listeners?"

"You have," said the Pooka, "and I'm trying to do it!"

"I want to ask Angus a question," said Ballor's Son, pushing forward.

"Ask it through me," said the Pooka. "Angus is a poet: and about a million years hence in that part of Chaos known as the Civilized World, poets will have typists and stenographers and private secretaries to protect them. Angus has only me. What do you want of him?"

"I want some Good Advice," said Ballor's Son.

"You should ask rather for a Good Example," said the Pooka, "it is better than Good Advice."

"I want to know how I can earn my living here in this Country of the Ever-Young."

"This is a serious matter," said the Pooka, "you must have a Craft of some kind: and Angus is the one to tell you of it, for a poet is the Master of Every Craft."

"I don't want to be a poet," said Ballor's Son.

"You couldn't look like a poet if you tried," said the Pooka, "but you might learn a few useful and amusing conjuring tricks, and go about showing them – if only you lived in the Civilized World you could be an advertisement of some kind."

"I'd like to try the conjuring tricks."

"Well," said the Pooka, "look at me, and copy my actions. First I shake my right ear and bend the tip of it."

The Pooka shook his tufted right ear and bent the tip of it.

Ballor's Son tried to shake his right ear and bend the tip of it, but he only shook his head and shook his head, and nothing happened. "It can't be done!" said Ballor's Son.

"What are your hands for?" cried Angus. "Look at me," and he put his hand to his right ear and shook it and bent the tip.

"I'll do that!" cried Ballor's Son, and he grasped his right ear firmly and shook it; but when he thought to bend the tip, the ear came off in his hand!

"Was there ever such a Child of Misfortune," cried the Pooka, "don't you know that the Land of the Ever-Young isn't adamant and iron like

Ballor's country? You must touch things gently. You must barely touch them at all! You should just have beckoned to that ear of yours with one finger!"

"Boo-hoo – hoo – hoo!" wailed Ballor's Son.

"Stop that unseemly noise," said Angus, "you have nothing to cry about. Just feel the side of your head again."

He caught the luckless right hand of Ballor's Son and pressed it against the right-hand side of his head: and, sure enough, Ballor's Son felt his right ear back again in its place!

"Angus," said the Pooka, "don't you think he should have a strong-man's Craft? Something with hammering in it, or yanking trees up by the roots?"

"We can't let him hurt the feelings of a tree," said Angus, "but he can be a blacksmith, and hammer iron. He can shoe horses."

"Yes," said Ballor's Son, "I would like to shoe horses."

"Well," said the Pooka, "Angus will help you to it:

"Shut your eyes,
  Turn three times to your right,
  Turn three times to your left,
  Rub your nose:
  Stamp three times with your right foot,
  Stamp three times with your left foot,
  Open your eyes
  And see what fortune has sent you!"

When Ballor's Son had turned about, just like the Pooka told him; and stamped with his feet, just like the Pooka told him; and opened his eyes, he saw Angus with nothing on but a tanned ox-hide hammering at a smith's anvil: and the Pooka, who had turned himself into a shock-headed boy, blowing the fire for him.

Angus showed Ballor's Son how to soften iron in the fire, how to hammer it into shape, how to plunge it hissing into water to harden it. He taught him also a little song such as smiths use to lighten their work:

"Ding dong dithero
  Ding dong doo:
  Have you a mare to shoe?
  You have –
  Then bring her hither O

Ding dong dithero
Ding dong doe."

"Now," said Angus, "you know how to fashion a shoe: we need a small pony or a little small-footed burro for you to shoe."

"I want a great big horse," said Ballor's Son.

"You hear that, Pooka," said Angus, "you better change yourself into the biggest Kelpie you can think of!"

"What's a Kelpie?" asked Ballor's Son.

"A Kelpie looks exactly like a horse," said Angus, "but it can plunge to the bottom of the sea, and live under water as easily as on dry land. If you can shoe a Kelpie you can shoe anything."

"Oh, please, good Pooka, change yourself," said Ballor's Son.

The Pooka clapped his hands together and made a high leap in the air. When he came down he was a most enormous great big white horse. His eyes were blue like ice, and his tail swept like a cloud about him.

"Now, you see a Kelpie," said Angus.

The Kelpie snorted and cavorted, he kicked up multitudinous sods of earth, he tossed his mane till it looked like a breaking sea-wave, and he blew spume out of his nostrils.

"He looks bigger than I wanted him to be," said Ballor's Son. "Can't Flame of Joy shoe him?"

"No," said Angus, "you must shoe him: but if you put one shoe on him it will be enough."

"Angus," said the Pooka-Kelpie, "I'm not sure that I want to be shod at all. It might spoil my uselessness – and that's the chief thing about me!"

"Pooka," said Angus, "have no fear of that: your uselessness is colossal. You will win rather a new dominion; for, if you have one decent shoe, you can gain a footing in the Civilized World: you can step from myth to literature. People will make statues of you and write books about you. They will call you Bucephalus – Bellerophim – Heliopolis – Higgograff –"

"That's enough at one time," said the Pooka.

"Pooka," said Angus, "those names are like chunks of amber. You could make a necklace of those names. You could hang one of those names in each of your ears for an ornament and a thing of wonder and beauty!"

"How do you spell them?" asked Ballor's Son.

"Never mind that, just now," said Angus, "your business is to shoe the Kelpie. Flame of Joy can hold him for you."

"But you are to teach me how," said Ballor's Son, "and how can you teach me if you don't put on the shoe yourself? A Good Example is better than Good Advice."

"Your wits show signs of sharpening," said Angus. "I will put the shoe on the Kelpie, and you shall hammer in the nails."

That was how they managed it, and when the Kelpie had one good shoe well-fitted to his foot, Angus said:

"Son of Ballor, I give you fire, anvil and iron: and Flame of Joy to act as helper. Try your luck! Come, Pooka, we are needed elsewhere."

"Angus," said the Pooka, "you have a heart of adamant, but I am compassionate. I am going to stay here and help Ballor's Son with some Good Advice when the next animal comes to be shod."

Angus laughed and walked away, but the Pooka changed himself back again into a cat. This time his fur was blue, barred and spotted with black. His ears had long black tufts on them, and his tail had a black tuft at the end: his claws shone like burnished onyx. He sat by the anvil where the firelight flickered on him.

It seemed to Ballor's Son that a very long time went past before anyone came to ask craftsmanship from the master of the forge under the apple trees. Dusk was purpling the shadows when at length he caught sight of a young man and a strange beast approaching. The man was slender of body and handsome, a straight robe clung to him from head to foot and the jewels on it winked and glittered as he walked: his golden shoes curled upward at the toe and walked daintily. He held a rose in one hand and the other hand rested on the neck of the strange beast – a beast that might have been taken for a horse only for the long straight horn growing out from its forehead.

"My Heart Within," cried Flame of Joy, "here comes one in search of a craftsman."

"Tell me, what is that beast?" said Ballor's Son, almost under his breath.

"It is a Unicorn," said Flame of Joy, "and this is a Persian Poet walking in a dream a thousand years hence. Speak softly for presently he will ask us to shoe the Unicorn."

The Unicorn was very white. It walked more daintily than the Poet, and as it walked it looked sidelong. Its eyes were green as emerald stones.

"I don't like the looks of him at all," said Ballor's Son, "I won't shoe him. He can stab with his horn, he can bite and kick and gore all at the same time. Tell him to go away!"

"The Poet will quiet him," said the Pooka, "he'll only need to speak a verse out of one of his own poems and the Unicorn will go to sleep."

The Poet and the Unicorn came slowly up to the forge under the apple tree and when they were close to it they stood still.

"I have enticed this Beautiful One," said the Poet, "from the Garden of the Moon-Goddess where he glittered between the trees like a white lotus between the trees like a white lotus between reed-stems in a pool of silent waters."

The Unicorn closed his green eyes and went to sleep.

"Don't you want me to shoe him?" cried Ballor's Son. "I'm ready to do it: I can do it at once."

"Have you the wherewithal to do it in seemly fashion?" asked the Poet.

"I have fire, anvil, and iron, if that's what you mean."

"Iron," said the Poet in a weary scornful voice, "is that a metal pleasing to the Moon? You are neither Alchemist nor Astrologer; else you would know that Aries rules that heavy sullen wounding metal. I will seek a master-forger elsewhere."

"Lord of a Thousand Pearls of Song," cried the Pooka, "Do not leave us! The knowledge you require is with me. I am the poor household cat of the Illustrious Smith. He instructed me in the sciences of astrology and alchemy when I was as yet but a six weeks' kitten and I have treasured this wisdom which he, under the stress of great knowledge, has forgotten. I know well that silver is the metal pleasing to the Moon-Goddess."

"What do you mean by saying that?" asked Ballor's Son, in a whisper, "We haven't any silver."

"The Poet has," said the Pooka, in another whisper.

"Of silver, then," said the Poet, "you shall hammer the shoes."

"Rose of the Civilized World," said the Pooka, "plain silver is all unworthy. It must be silver that you have sanctified and incensed with the breath of poetry. So clever is this Smith that out of your finger-ring he can hammer shoes."

The Poet took from his finger a silver ring with a moonstone set in it.

"Of this silver," he said, "You shall hammer the shoes."

Ballor's Son hammered and hammered till he had a shoe so slender and so delicately fashioned that you could hardly see it.

"Now," he said. "I will shoe the Unicorn."

Flame of Joy lifted the Unicorn's hind foot very gently, and Ballor's Son fitted the shoe to it, but when he drove the first nail the Unicorn woke up and kicked him into the apple tree. And the Unicorn wasn't even satisfied with this: he tore Flame of Joy's tunic with his teeth, and he tried to stab the Pooka with his horn. The Pooka somersaulted in the air and came down on his four feet, the way a cat always does.

"O Fierce Beautiful Energy," cried the Poet, "O Divine One, I love the lovely motions of your head, the lovelier rhythms of your feet!"

The Unicorn closed his green eyes and slept.

"Now," said the Pooka to Ballor's Son, "try again!"

"I won't," said Ballor's Son, "I won't come within hoof-reach of him, even if I never earn my living!"

"If that be so," said the Poet, "it is needless for us to tarry longer."

"O Sweet-tongued Magician," said the Pooka, "if anyone can shoe your Unicorn, this Smith can do it. Only you must continue to recite poetry till the last shoe-nail is in place."

"I might recite my epic," said the Poet.

"O Lord of Wisdom," cried the Pooka, "you have found the remedy. Recite your epic."

The Poet began the recitation, and with every word the sleeping Unicorn went deeper and deeper into himself till he seemed to be sleeping himself out of his body.

"Be quick, now, Ballor's Son," cried the Pooka, "and shoe him before he melts away. Can't you see that he is growing diaphanous with ecstasy! Even a Unicorn cannot stand a whole epic!"

Ballor's Son edged cautiously up to the Unicorn. Flame of Joy lifted his hind foot very gently. Ballor's Son fitted the silver shoe to it, and all might have gone well if he hadn't overbalanced himself trying to drive a nail without hitting it! He clutched, my grief, at the Unicorn's long thick tail to steady himself – and there was no strength or substance in that tail! His hand went through it as if it were no more than a wisp of moonshine. And he didn't save himself from falling: he came against the Unicorn's hindquarters and found that he was leaning on nothingness. The Unicorn was crumpling up. He was vanishing like mist. Soon even the shadow of him was not there.

Ballor's Son sat down with violent and unnecessary suddenness.

The Persian Poet turned startled eyes on him, and the rose dropped delicately from his fingers. He made a gesture of farewell. Ballor's Son clung frantically to the embroidered robe.

"Bring him back," he cried, "bring back the Unicorn!"

But the Persian Poet shook his head, smiling wanly: and Ballor's Son saw that he too was fading into nothingness. He clutched more strongly at him, but there was no substance to hold to; there was nothing but a voice, almost bodiless, echoing languorous and scornful out of nowhere:

"Alas, my heart, how thin a stuff our dreams are made of!"

"I hope you're proud of yourself!" cried Flame of Joy, stamping about and dancing with rage, "I hope you're proud of yourself, treating a Unicorn like a common Kyelin or any of the quadrupeds in your own sun-forsaken, moon-forgotten country! I hope you're proud of yourself!"

The Pooka had not moved from his place by the anvil with the firelight flickering on him. He smiled and smiled silently to himself, the way a cat smiles when it doesn't want to hurt the feelings of a big lumbering stupid-minded human being. Ballor's Son sat down beside the Pooka and sobbed and sobbed and sobbed. He sobbed unrestrainedly, and after a while he didn't know what he was sobbing for or where he was: and when he stopped sobbing he found himself in his own bed at home with the First Lord-in-Waiting sitting solemnly at the head, and the Second Lord-in-Waiting at the foot.

Ballor's Son sat upright amongst his pillows. He seized his head with both hands as if to keep it from flying into space with the stress of his thinking: and with the stress of his thinking the hair on the top of his head rose in a point!

POEMS FROM
MARZILIAN
(1938)

In this collection of poetry Ella Young explored themes that were an important part of her inner landscape throughout her life. Magic, the mystery of life itself, the natural world and our relationship to it, and above all the wonderful figures of myth and legend, folklore and ancient literature who were old friends from her earliest reading. All are tinged with a certain sadness, as though the poet knows that such delights are being forgotten or neglected in the time she lived. This makes her celebration of Irish myth, Arthurian legend and magic even more poignant for us today – who have moved even further from the world of delight to be found in these stories – though we are, perhaps, finally beginning to rediscover them.

VALUES

What shall we say of the rose?
Petal by petal it goes
A-swirl in the dust.

What of the sword?
By the side of a slain knight it knows
The durance of rust.

And what of the word:
Poet's song, or the song of a bird?
Silence is lord.

What of the star
In heaven's blue arras-cloth,
Should flame be a bar?
Ask the moth!

GRAMMARYE

Riding through the shadowed wood
Three queens came to where I stood –
By the blossoming twisted thorn!

Said the first queen, *"Gold is fair,"*
Sun-bright gold her wind-blown hair.

Said the second, *"Blood is red,"*
And she was pale as one that's dead.

The third said, *"Long sleep is good,"*

So those three queens rode through the wood,
And it was early morn.

SARRAS-CITY

Sarras built to flaunt the sky
Brazen towers uplifted high,
So proud a vaunt she made,
So stout her heart to dare:
Like an aureole displayed
Her banners were.

No lover is left her now to tell
Of the splendour that she had,
The riot of days half-mad:
No one to pause, or pass,
No one to cry *"Alas"!*
In all her streets. Her glittering towers fell.

ARBOR VITÆ

There swings a branch
By the High Queen's dune
Down far below the sea,
It is silver-bright with blossom and fruit
For the High Queen's self to see:
And every maker of verse and rann,
Every poet since time began,
Has toiled and longed to be
Where he might taste of the magical fruit,
Or pluck one leaf from the tree.
But only those who have said farewell to the sun
May come to the dune by the Silver Tree,
And find in hollow or height
Under the still green tideless sea
The Rose of Silence and Night.

ENDYMION THE SHEPHERD TO THE MOON-QUEEN ARTEMIS

You come no more.
The voices of the night
Sink into silence.
Soon broad day will stare
Between the tree-tops, mocking at my grief.
My own heart mocks me: why should you look down,
White Artemis, with all the windy plain
Of the skies to hunt in, why should you look down
Remembering a shepherd of the hills?
Follow the red-eared tireless hound! Farewell.

Yet, if immortal beauty can take aught
That mortal hands would proffer, take with you
A memory of these woods, of silences
More sweet than sound, of all sweet things that die:
So shall another lover, loving you,
Touch hearts with me, Endymion, unaware.

A SONG THAT TROSTAN MADE

If I were a king's son
I would give you a white hound
In a leash of silver,
I would give you a white stallion
From over the sea.
I would give you a cloak of purple
Wrought with findruiny,
And shoes of white bronze,
If I were a king's son.

You would talk with me
In the bright-coloured palace:
You would be glad at my coming,
If I were a king's son.

FIONAVAR

O flame blown out of Tir-nan-Oge,
White flame borne on enchanted air,
O heart's delight and heart's despair,
Fionavar! O Fionavar!

Draw the white shroud above her face
And cover up her close-shut eyes,
She will not hear a voice that cries
Fionavar! O Fionavar!

Love that none of us might win,
By strange lone ways to us you came
And lone you go, White Heart of Flame,
Fionavar! O Fionavar!

Pale face that held our hearts in thrall,
Pale face made paler by our love,
We could but draw the shroud above,
Fionavar! O Fionavar!

47

Frail hands no mortal lover kissed,
Fair-folded now as death beseems,
You hide away the Dream of Dreams,
Fionavar! O Fionavar!

WHITE HORSES

White horses the sea has,
Dead men dream of them
Under the waters.

Whiter than moon-fire they glitter
In a wave leaping shoreward;
They neigh in the storm-wind
They cry to each other
White as the levin-flash
Sudden and splendid.

White horses the sea has;
Under the waters
Dead men dream of them.

AN OLD SONG

My sorrow on the breaking wave
That breaks, and leaves the shore:
Black bitter sorrow for my Love
Beyond me evermore.

The sea draws back its wave again,
The white moon draws the sea:
And I would reach unto my Love
If only I were free.

Ella Young's Sacred Mount Shasta, 2006.
Photograph by Peter Reichelt Hughes.

SHASTA

Mountain that jewels the morning,
Snow-ermined, star-crowned at night,
Throned, yet the throneless unscorning,
Mother and Maid of Delight,
Lean to us, hear us, we make
A word, a song for your sake.

Like shaken sand in a glass
The years, the centuries run,
You are young, nor out-wearied at all
With your comrade the sun:
We are clouds that drift and must go,
Leaves that tremble and fall,
Shadows that pass,
O Mother, O Maiden, you know
Us and the flowers in the grass.

You hear the star-flocks singing
A proud song and high;
Hear us, our hearts too are winging
A song going by.
The star-song will last while you live:
We have but little to give,
Who see you and die.

Cry of the eagle,
Moan of the dove,
Falcon wing in the sky,
Of these and blossoms we make
A Word, a song for your sake;
We pray you have joy thereof,
As you joy in the star-song high:
Have joy in one and the other,
Maiden and Mother
When we no longer go by.

Lotus of Dawnlight,
Beautiful, pure,
Through the long centuries
Blossom, endure.

TRIPTYCH

It is rumoured that folk in the Faery-World have power to charm the souls of such as are inclined to them forth from their bodies in sleep and take them a-journeying in strange lands.

– Book of the Opal

1: Wave Blossom

They plunge on the sea-marge,
Their proud heads a-toss,
Horses from Faeryland.

Awake, awake, and ride with me,
Laughing and light as a wave of the sea.
Swift as the flight of a swallow:
Our horses champ and chafe in the spray,
Come away — away!

Sea-voices call us,
Voices of water and night,
Song of the running wave
And the wave up-clomb,
Thunder of surf breaking free,
Breaking free!

The maiden moon has snared the sea
In a noose, in a net of chalcedony:
With a song she draws the shore-wave home
In glinting fire, in sounding foam.
Home with the wave,
The wind-swung wave,
The glinting wave,
Go we
All so merrily riding:

Through water green as chrysoprase
(Moon-pale we on horses white,)
Through water green as malachite,
(The way our proud steeds know,)
There is lapis gold below:
All gay of heart, so gay, we go,
Chasing the light a-sliding
Scimitar-curved in the wave-trough's gloom,
Racing the moon in pool and shallow
To the crested wave-plume;

Climbing, climbing,
With the wave up-heaping
To meet the sky;
With the dolphins leaping,
In silver crescents sweeping,
Low and high:

While the mer-folk slender fair,
Sweet of voice as birds in air,
Lift their lovely heads and dare
To keep pace with us unknowing
Whence we came or whither going:
Glancing,
Glittering
From peak to hollow,
Foam-white
Bubble-light
Bubble-free to follow.

Follow, O follow, follow,
Folk of the Sea,
Follow us!

Mer-folk now the sea caresses,
Winding their long tresses
A-down, a-down, and deeper yet,
Their long tresses,
Where no star is met,
Not a star to heed
How they swirl with the water-weed,
Candling the deep.

Music of mer-folk singing,
Like bronze bells set a-swinging
From wave to wave height ringing:
Wild music of their laughter
Luring behemoth after,
Luring the Lords of the Sea;
Till lulled and charmed each leaning head
Longs for a country laughter-fed,
Land-Under-Wave where no storm lowers.
Land of the scarlet lily flowers.

We sink like sea-mew sliding,
Like a shadow gliding
Down where light so still is
To the Land of Red Lilies,
To the Forest of Wonder
Under the sea-wave,
The deep sea-surge under.

Hark, how they stamp, at the sea-marge,
Neighing,
Horses from Faeryland
Pawing a-chafe in the spray:
Awake! Awake, come away!

2: Moon Flame

The lotus wakens in the pool,
The moon wakes in the skies;
Shake the deep slumber from your heart,
The slumber from your eyes.

The wind's a hound to run all night
Shadowed in silver and pearl;
Ours are the stars for candle-light.
Till the dawn-song of the merle.

Bind your hair in a golden net,
Slip from the sleep-fast clay:
We have till the shrill-throated cocks
Cry in the whitening day.

O hasten, for the moon will set,
Will set too soon,
Bind your heavy hair in a net
Glimmering like the moon.

3: Land Under Wave

Hawk in highest air,
Feathered snow-flake we,
Light as blown rose-petals are.
And like rose-petals blown,
Thistle-down set free,
Or golden leaves from a tree,
Dizzying up the sky
Star swirls on star
As we plunge by:
The moon's a lotus whirled and tossed,
Whirled — and lost!

Foam of stars about us now:
Sea-foam, salt-stinging.

Sea-spray up-flinging
A blossomed bough!

The Wave!
The Wave!
O'er-toppling,
White;
Cavernous
As the mouth of Night.

It draws us down,
Down, down,
To the sound of a bell,
(A great bell swinging,)
Down to Moy-Mell,
To the Honey-Plain,
The Land of Heart's Delight,
So lost, so long desired in vain.

Neither sun nor moon
Troubles this still air
Where light of night and noon
Is interfused and fair.

Here joy the heart entrances,
And care may not suborn:
Here where Lilith dances
So light beneath the Thorn.

Trees were for Lilith appled,
And dark pomegranate boughs,
Where a unicorn all silver
Might lift a head to browse.

She sings the stars to roses,
The moon to starry rain;
The sun, a lotus, closes,
Nor wakes again.

And still the scarlet lilies
Are joyous in this place,
Deep-drowsed and honey-hearted
With Lilith's face.

Among the scarlet lilies
We ride with dream-fast eyes,
We ride among the lilies
Until the dawn-cock cries:

Cries-in the Morn, with eager throat,
And on that clarion note,
So chill, so piercing clear,
Loveliness falters here,
Like a tear-drop shaken
From eyes unfain to waken,
Loveliness falters here,
Turmoil of earth draws near.
Banishing Paradise!

O lightly lightly here
Our white steeds go,
Lighter than drifting snow
In the net of the wind-god drawn,
Light as a leaf before the dawn,

Light as a leaf in Paradise,
Until the grey cock cries,
Cries Morn on garth and lawn,
Bleak Morn upon our eyes,
On our dream-cloistered eyes
The turbulent red of dawn
Banishing Paradise.

THE WONDER SMITH AND HIS SON
(1927)

In this selection from Ella Young's 1927 collection we are introduced to the figure of the Gubbaun Saor, a character familiar to students of Celtic mythology. They have the feel of folk tales rather than high epic or grand myth, but they are still powerful explorations of a time and way of life, echoes of which could still be felt when Ella Young was growing up in Ireland. There is a beauty and sweetness about them, occasionally tempered with humour that is rare in modern literature but very much a part of the stories of the elder days. These stories actually comprise an extended sequence, but there are sufficient stand-alone episodes to read as they are presented here. We have included six out of the fourteen stories that make up the original book.

HOW THE GUBBAUN SAOR GOT HIS TRADE

It was drawing towards night, and the Gubbaun had not given a thought to his sleeping place. All about him was sky, and a country that looked as if the People of the Gods of Dana had been casting shoulder-stones in it since the beginning of time. As far as the Gubbaun's eyes travelled there was nothing but stone; grey stone, silver stone, stone with veins of crystal and amethyst, stone that was purple to blackness; tussocks and mounds of stone; plateaus and crags and jutting peaks of stone; wide endless, spreading deserts of stone. Like a jagged cloud, far-off, a city climbed the horizon.

The Gubbaun sat down. He drew a barley-cake from his wallet, and some cresses. He ate his fill and stretched himself to sleep.

The pallor of dawn was in the air when a shriek tore the sleep from him. He sat up: great wings beat the sky making darkness above him, and something dropped to the earth within hand-reach. He fingered it –

a bag of tools! As he touched them he knew that he had skill to use them though his hands had never hardened under a tool in his life. He slung the wallet on his shoulder and set off towards the town.

As he neared it he was aware of a commotion among the townsfolk – they ran hither and thither; they stared at the sky; they clung together in groups.

"What has happened to your town?" said the Gubbaun to a man he met.

"A great misfortune has happened," said the man. "This town, as you can see, has the noblest buildings in the world: poets have made songs about this town. This town is itself a song, a boast, splendour, a cry of astonishment! Men wonder at this town. The djinns, craning from battlemented storm-winds, have no pride left in them: they are shamefaced before this town.

"Three Master-Builders came to this town – builders that had not their fellows on the ridge of the world. They set themselves to the making of a Marvel; a Wonder of Wonders; a Cause of Astonishment and Envy; a Jewel; a Masterpiece in this town of masterpieces – this place that is jewelled like the Tree of Heaven and drunken with Marvels!

"One pact alone, one obligation they bound with oath on the townsfolk – no living person was to come within the enclosure where they worked; no living person – man, woman, or child – was to set eyes on them when they passed through the town with the tools of their trade in their hands.

"It was *Geas* for them to be looked on.

"We cloaked our eyes when they passed, we darkened our windows when they passed, we closed our doors.

"Three days they were working and passing through the town with the tools of their trade. We had contentment, and luck and prosperity, till the whitening of this dawn. Then a red-polled woman thrust her head forth – my curse on the breed and seed of her for seven generations – she set the edge of her eyes on the Three Master-Builders. They let a screech out of them and rose in the air. They put the shapes of birds on themselves and flew away – my grief, three black crows!

"Now the stone waits for the hammer: and the hammer is lost with the hand that held it!"

The Gubbaun tightened his grasp on the wallet, and his feet took him of their own accord away from the town.

"The tools have come to the man who can handle them," said the Gubbaun to himself: "but I'll handle them for the first time where there are fewer tongues to wag."

HOW THE GUBBAUN PROVED HIMSELF

The Gubbaun wandered at his own will, as the wind wanders. Everyplace seemed good to him, because his heart was happy.

He sat by a river cataract and watched the leap of a great king-salmon, silver against the swirling flood.

"My blessing on you, Brother," he cried, "and your own heart's wish to you." With that a Pooka lifted himself head and shoulders from the spume. He had put the shape of a white stallion on himself. His eyes were blue like ice.

"If you blessed me," he said, "I could take you to the Land-Under-Wave, to the Plain with Red Blossoms."

"I know that Plain," said the Gubbaun; "but it is work on the world-ridge that I am seeking now. I would prove myself and my tools."

"The sun and wind, the rain and hail, will eat into your work. Old age will gnaw at the roots of it. Put your hand on my neck, and your blessing on me!"

"My blessing to you, Brother of mine; White Love of Running Water; White Wave of the Turbulent Sea. I will win you lovers and new kingdoms. You shall be a song in the heart; a dream that slips from city to city; a flame; a whiteness of peace in the murk of battle; a honeyed laughter; a quenchless delight. These, O my Brother, because of me: and at the last, my hand upon your neck."

"Call, and I follow," said the Pooka:

"I am a Hound whiter than the sun.
A Stag I am with golden antlers.
A Tree I am with silver fruit.
A Voice in the wind's voice I am.
I am running water and growing grass.

Take my blessing, Master-Builder; take my blessing, Wonder-Smith."

"If I am sun to-day, and you the shadow," said the Gubbaun, "tomorrow you are sun, and I the shadow. Day in, day out, let there be love between us and no farewell."

The Gubbaun shouldered his tools. Walking at his will, he came to a place where a great chief's dune was a-building. The folk that fashioned it were disputing and arguing among themselves.

"It is right," said one who had an air of authority and a red cloak on him; "it is right that on this lintel there should be an emblem to show the power of the lord of the dune – an emblem to put loosening of joints and terror upon evil-doers."

"It is more fitting," said another, "that the man who carves the emblem should be honoured in it."

"Nay," said a third, "the man who raised the stone should be honoured in it. I myself should be honoured."

So the clash of tongues and opinions went on.

"The blessing of the sun, and the colours of the day to you," said the Gubbaun. "Have ye work for a Craftsman?"

"What Craftsman are you," said they, "that come hither a-begging? The world runs after the Master-Craftsman – we have no need of bunglers!"

"I am a Master-Craftsman."

"Hear him!" cried they all. "Where are your apprentices? What dunes have you built? What jewels have you carved? Tell us that!"

"A man with ill-cobbled brogues, and burrs in his coat – a likely lie!"

"Put me to the proof," said the Gubbaun, "set me a task!"

"So vagrants talk," said the man in the red cloak, "while good men sweat at labour. Have you the hands of a mason?"

"What need to waste wit and words on this churl?" cried another. "It is time now to stretch our limbs in the sun, and to eat. Let us go to the stream where the cresses are."

They went.

When they were well out of the way, the Gubbaun took his tools. He worked with a will. The work was finished when they straggled back.

The first that caught sight of it cried out: the cry ran from man to man of them.

There was hand-clapping and amazement.

The Gubbaun had carved the King-Cat: Keshcorran – more terrible than a tiger! The Cat crouched midway in the lintel, and on either side of him spread a tail, a tail worthy that Royal One! Bristling with fierceness it spread; it slid along on either side, with insinuating grace and with infinite cunning, losing itself at the last in loops, and twists, and foliations and intricacies that spread and returned and established themselves in a mysterious, magical, spell-knotted forest of emblems behind the flat-eared threatening head.

"There is an emblem for the Builder in that," said the Gubbaun, "and an emblem for the Carver, and an emblem for the Man who Planned the Dune, and for the Earth that gave the stone for it. Is it enough?"

"It is enough, O Master-Craftsman, our Choice you are! Our Share of Luck you are! Our treasure! Stay with us. The chief seat in our assembly shall be yours. The chief voice in our council shall be yours. Stay with us, Royal Craftsman."

"I have the wisdom of running water and growing grass," said the Gubbaun, "and my feet must carry me further – still water is stagnant! May every day bring laughter to your mouths, and skill to your fingers; may the cloaks of night bring wisdom."

He left them.

Often he was wandering after that when the sun was proud in the sky – and often when the sun was under the earth. He drank honey-mead in Faery-Mounds. He saw the Mountain-Sprites dancing. At last he built a noble habitation for the one daughter that he had and for himself. Aunya was the daughter's name. She had the cleverness of her father, but the Gubbaun's heart was set on a son.

HOW THE SON OF THE GUBBAUN MET WITH GOOD LUCK

"It would be well for you to be raising a hand on your own behalf, now," said the Gubbaun Saor to his Son, you can draw the birds from the bushes with one note of your flute: maybe you can draw luck with a woman. If you have the luck to get the daughter I gave in exchange for yourself, our good days will begin."

The Son of the Gubbaun got to his feet.

"I could travel the world," he said, "with my reed-flute and the Hound that came to me out of the Wood of Gold and Silver Yew Trees." With that he gave a call, and a milk-white Hound came running to the door.

"Is it without counsel and without advice and without a road-blessing," cried the Gubbaun, "that you are setting out to travel the world? How will you know what girl has the fire of wisdom in her mind? What sign, what token will you ask of her?"

"'Tis you that have wisdom: give me an advice," said the Son.

"Take the sheepskin," said the Gubbaun, "and set yourself to find a buyer for it. The girl that will give you the skin and the price of it is the girl that will bring good-luck across this threshold. The day and the hour that you find her, send home the Hound that I may know of her and set out the riches of this house."

"Tree of Wisdom," said the Son, "bear fruit and blossom on your branches. The road blessing now to me."

"My blessing on the road that is smooth," said the Gubbaun, "and on the rough road through the quagmire. A blessing on night with the stars; and night when the stars are quenched. A blessing on the clear sky of day; and day that is choked with the thunder. May my blessing run before you. May my blessing guard you on the right hand and on the left. May my blessing follow you as your shadow follows. Take my road-blessing," said the Gubbaun.

"The shelter of the Hazel Boughs to you, Salmon of Wisdom," said the Son.

He set out then with the Hound to travel the solitary places and the marts of the world. He shook the dust of many a town from his feet, but the sheepskin remained on his shoulder. A cause of merriment that skin was; a target for shafts of wit; a shaming of face to the man that carried it. It found its way into proverbs and wonder tales, but it never found the bargain-clinch of a buyer.

If it hadn't been for the Hound, and the reed-flute, and the share of songs that he had, the Son of the Gubbaun Saor would have been worn to a skin of misery like a dried-up crab apple!

One day, in the teeth of the North Wind, he climbed a hill-gap and came all at once on a green plain. There was only one tree in that plain, but everywhere scarlet blossoms trembled through the grass. Beneath the tree was a well: and from the well a girl came towards him. Her heavy hair was like spun gold. She walked lightly and proudly. The Son of the Gubbaun thought it long till he could change words with her.

"May every day bring luck and blessing to you," he cried.

"The like wish to yourself," said she, "and may your load be light."

"A good wish," said he, "I have far to carry my load."

"How far?" asked the girl.

"To the world's end, I think."

"Are you under enchantment?" said she. "Did a Hag of the Storm put a spell on you; or a Faery-Woman take you in her net?"

"'Tis the net of my father's wisdom that I am caught in," said he. "I must carry this sheepskin, my grief! till a woman gives me the price of it: and the skin itself, in the clinch of a good buyer's bargain."

"You need go no farther for that," said the girl. "Name your price for the skin."

He named his price. She took the skin. She plucked the wool from it. She gave him the skin and the price together.

"Luck on your hand," said he, "is the bargain a good one?"

"It is," said she, "I have fine pure wool for the price of a skin. May the price be a luck-penny! "

"You are the Woman my father brags of," cried the Son. "My Choice, My Share of the World you are, if you will come with me."

"I will come," said the girl.

The Son of the Gubbaun Saor called to the Hound.

"Swift One," he said, "our fortunes have blossomed. Set out now, and don't let the wind that is behind you catch you up, or the wind that is in front of you outrace you, till you lie down by the Gubbaun Saor's threshold."

The Hound stretched himself in his running. He was like a salmon that silvers in mid-leap; like the wind through a forest of sedges; like the sun-track on dark waters: and he was like that in his running till he lay down by the Gubbaun Saor's threshold.

THE BUILDING OF BALOR'S DUNE

At the edge of the Black Waters two of Balor's lords awaited the Gubbaun and his Son. They were cloaked and hooded and closely masked, yet it seemed to the Son of the Gubbaun that under the hood of one of them there was only half a face, and under the hood of the other the head of some strange animal.

"Salutation," said the half-faced one, and as he spoke the sea of black waters reared itself in waves. "Salutation to the Wonder-Smith and his Son. I am Hrut of the many shapes, the son of Sruth, the son of Sru, the son of Nar, chief and man of might in the country of Balor – and lo, Balor's boat awaits us!"

Beneath them, huddling against a jagged stairway, a boat lay blackly on the Black Waters. It had neither steersman nor galley-slave, neither sail nor oar. Unmoored it swung blankly like a drowned body cast up by the sea.

Without a word the Gubbaun stepped aboard. The Son followed. The hooded lords took their places. Hrut leaned over the stern. He lifted three handfuls of water and flung them against the sky. He gave a loud, piercing, horrible cry.

At that a sea-demon put his shoulder to the boat. He lifted the sea in a curved black foam-smoking precipice in front of the prow – he left it a gaping hollow behind! Short was their crossing.

Harsh was their welcome in Balor's country. A hard bleak desolate wilderness Balor's country was. The sun never lifted his forehead on it. The moon never showed herself. Every blade of grass in Balor's country was like a knife with a drop of venom on the point of it. The jagged stones were scimitar-edged.

"Will it please you, Wonder-Smith, to walk or ride?" asked Hrut.

"To ride," said the Gubbaun.

Hrut gave a keen piercing cry.

Down THEY swooped out of the air; horribly toothed and clawed, with wings that made a storm about them. Fire came from their nostrils. They bit and clawed one another.

"Will you ride, Wonder-Smith?" asked Hrut.

"I will ride," said the Gubbaun, "put bridles on them."

They put bridles on the biggest one for the Gubbaun, and on the second biggest one for the Son.

"Have you rods," said the Gubbaun, "to encourage them, or to chastise them?"

"They encourage themselves," said Hrut, "No rider has chastised them. Hold fast. As for us we will trust to our feet."

The Gubbaun took a master-grip. The Son copied him. They rose in the air.

"Oh!" cried the Son, "it is nothing I have under me but a slanting icy wind, and that is thinning and spreading away – I am falling!"

"Give your fine steed the rod," said the Gubbaun, "the Hazel rod!"

The Son of the Gubbaun Saor drew a blow on the wind, and with that the scaly-writhing, fire-breathing, feathered monster took shape under him again. It was so till they struck the fastness of Balor.

Balor's devastating eye was close shut. Hugely the eyelid weighed upon it, fleshy and sullen. Runes and spells and charms and incantations were on that lid to keep it shut. Balor's face was a blankness. His voice whipped the ears like sleet.

"Build me a dune," he said, "strong as the foundations of the earth; a dune with courts and passages and secret chambers; with carvings on the walls of it and carved monsters in the crevices of it; a dune that climbs and blossoms in spires and twists and flame-like billowing curves and fantasies; such a dune as never from the beginning of days shaped itself on the ridge of the world. Gold ye shall have in plenty, and rich jewels and cloaks of honour. Ye shall stagger under the load of your riches. I, Balor, have said it."

"Such a dune," said the Gubbaun, "I can rear."

The Gubbaun and his Son set to work. They had djinns, and dwarfs, and giants, and goat-footed men, and demons of the air, and fabulous animals, and monstrous beings, and strange beasts to help them. The dune took shape, it grew. There was great delight on the Son of the Gubbaun. He wished with all his heart for a reed flute, but Balor's country was bare of reeds. At length he fashioned a flute of metal, and as he played on it in an idle hour, a woman of Fomor drew close to him. She was poor. She had known hardship. Wrapped in her mantle she held a young child. It was a little while before she spoke. She said:

"For my little son I pray your good will with the music you make. There is a wasting sickness on him and he has no delight in life."

"I will make a Music of Delight for him," said the Gubbaun's Son.

The child put his mother's cloak away from him and peered out. His face was dusky; he had prick ears like a faun; his hair was a black tangled bush standing upon his head; his eyes were golden-yellow and very bright, like the eyes a goat has. His eyes pleased the Son of the Gubbaun Saor.

"I will play Strength and Joy," he said.

Every day after that the Son of the Gubbaun made music for the Fomor woman and her child. He played away the sickness. He played till the child laughed and danced and tumbled over himself with delight. One day the woman was troubled.

"You have given life and delight to my child," she said. "To-day he can repay you. My son has one gift from his birth – he can hear the stir of a bird's wing at the other end of the world! No walls can shut a whisper from him: and he has heard a whisper about you. Balor will put you and your father to death when ye have made an end of building the dune, lest a dune the like of it be reared for another. Take counsel therefore with what wisdom is in you and go unharmed from this country."

The Son of the Gubbaun took that news to his father.

"I must think," said the Gubbaun, and he sat down.

The djinns sat down. The goat-footed ones sat down. The fabulous animals stretched themselves and licked their paws. There was a marvellous, munificent, soul-gratifying cessation of labour.

Balor's voice split the stillness.

"Let the Gubbaun come before me," he cried.

The Gubbaun came.

"The work has stopped," roared Balor. "Wherefore?"

"The work has stopped," said the Gubbaun, "because I am short of a tool that is lying under seven locks in my treasure-chest at home."

"Give the tokens and signs of that tool," said Balor, "my swiftest messenger shall speed for it!"

"I trust no hand but my own on the tools of my trade."

"Trust your own hand: my messenger shall bring the treasure-chest."

"The chest is bedded with the foundations of the house: it cannot be moved!"

"If the house holds to the chest," said Balor, "my messenger will haul it hither as a net hauls the dog-fish with the salmon."

He called to one of his most powerful djinns.

"Go," he said, "and bring the treasure-chest of the Wonder-Smith hither, though you should bring the ribs of the earth with it!"

"Live for ever, Magnificence," said the djinn, and was gone.

"He will not come back," said the Gubbaun Saor.

Balor writhed his lips in a scornful smile.

THE GUBBAUN SAOR'S FEAST

When the Gubbaun Saor and his Son set foot again in Ireland, the earth was glad at their coming: a Wave in the North reared itself and fell with a sound of clangourous bells and loud-voiced trumpets: a Wave in the East reared itself and fell with a sound of clashing cymbals and shrill-voiced flutes: a Wave in the South reared itself and fell with a sound of sweet singing voices mingling with and overmastering the sound of timpaun and cruit and bell-branch: and all along the islands of the West and the rocky inlets went a singing reedy whisper, "*Mananaun! Mananaun!*"

The rhythm of that welcoming music was a pulse of joy in the flowering grasses: the strong oaks knew it: the white bulls of the forest moved to it, tossing their moon-curved horns: it set the sea-hawks sliding down the wind, stooping in circles: it was a hand-clapping and a shout of laughter in the mountain torrents.

"A noble land and a good, is Ireland," said the Gubbaun, "my thousand blessings on it!"

Aunya made a great Feast of Welcome for them. From the four corners of the world folk came to the Feast: some that had praise-mouthed names and a proud lineage, and some that had a virtue in them of such a strange and subtle essence that it escaped a clamorous recognition. Harpers came, and sweet-voiced women, and men of learning. Kings' sons came to it riding upon white stallions with bells and apples of gold on their bridle reins and the tails and manes of the stallions dyed a crimson-purple; the workers in brass and copper, the proud makers of beautiful things came to it, and simple poor folk came with good-will in their hearts.

The Chief-Poet of Ireland came, with thirty princes in his train, a slender dark-visaged man, his hair, wound upon and bound with twists of gold, his singing-robe on his shoulders that only the Chief-Poet might wear: curiously, wrought it was of the feathers of bright-coloured birds. There was a king from the North, blue-eyed and huge of limb, he that was lord of dragon-prowed ships. There was a queen from the South, a woman that many poets had loved: she had a face radiant and pale like magnolia blossom, and eyes the colour of the sky when dusk empurples it – and everywhere she was the one Rose of Delight.

And there came from the Faery Hills three Cup-Bearers, clad in raiment redder than carbuncle, so beautiful it was a heart-ache to look upon them. They had unwithering youth: beautiful as the light behind the sea-wave – beautiful as the apple-bough beyond our reach!

Light-hearted and impish, in their companies and multitudes, the Sheeoga came – they the Small Folk of the mountain and the bog-land, the Good People who put mortals astray at the fading of the light: or, mindful of new-querned meal heaped in porringers for them and oblations of sweet milk, conduct wayfarers by sure paths across the marshes and craggy sea-frowning precipices – with laughter the Sheeoga came. They joined hands and danced round the house. Aunya sent them out a silver bowl brimmed with wine. Fast as they emptied it, it filled itself again. From hand to hand, from lip to lip they passed it, dancing – their laughter rang like silver bells about the house.

Within the Gubbaun's house the candles of a king's feast were lighted. The djinn was there – he had measured the length of his ears by the height of the door-lintel. The Great Vizier was there, uncobwebbed of the treasure-chest. Balor's Son was there, splendid in his robes of embassy. The Hound Failinis was there, and a Phoenix-Bird that came out of Tir-nan-oge.

The feast began: it went from lavishness to lavishness, it was jewelled with strangeness, as a daggerhilt is crusted with gems. Towards the close, the Gubbaun raised a great Cup of crystal in his hands. The wine in it shone like a ruby: it was wine of Moy-Mell.

"Drink!" he cried. "Let each one drink to the measure of his thirst: the Cup is a well of plenty, it renews itself. The Cup went from guest to guest, and each one that held that Marvel in his hands drank to the thing he desired to honour. When the Cup came to Balor's Son he rose up and said: *"To Balor the Munificent, and to the noble dune that is a-building!"*

The Cup flew into a thousand splinters. The wine ran down like blood.

"Dragon of Death!" cried Balor's Son, "what evil omen is this?"

"The venom of untruth has shattered the Cup," said the Gubbaun. "Balor's munificence was treachery. But not for this thing shall the Cup be destroyed." He gathered the fragments in his hand. "Let truth make it whole: *Balor plotted my death and the death of my Son when the dune was finished."*

The Cup became whole in the Gubbaun's hand.

"But," said Balor's Son, "in the presence of the lords and chiefs of the Fomor you named the Tool: you gave the Master-Word."

"I named my Tool," said the Gubbaun.

The Crooked—against crookedness.
The Twist—against a twist:
    and
The Twist—against treachery:

That Tool I needed: that Tool my hands can handle now.
I drink to the time when Balor will know that gods are not jealous of godhead!"

The Gubbaun drank till not a drop remained in the Cup.

"Tell Balor," he said, "that the envious heart drips poison on its own wounds, but munificence begets munificence. His mind imagined a palace: let him build it – he has the multitudinous centuries for leisure! But this one night is ours for joy and song. Let music sound, and let the jugglers now toss up the glittering balls."

Tulkinna the Peerless One stepped forward. He had nine golden apples and nine feathers of white silver and nine discs of findruiney. He tossed them up: they leaped like a plume of sea-spray, they shone like wind-stirred flame, they whirled like leaves rising and falling. He wove them into patterns. They danced like gauze-winged flies on a summer's eve. They gyrated like motes of dust. They tangled the mind in a web of light and darkness till at last it seemed that Tulkinna was tossing the stars.

Then came a burst of light-hearted music.
The djinn danced with the Phoenix-Bird.
Aunya danced with Balor's Son.
The Chief Vizier danced with a woman out of Tir-nan-oge.
The Gubbaun Saor's Son danced with the queen from the South.

The sun and moon, the stars and constellations, danced to the measure of that dancing. The memory of it was honey in the mind of poets for a thousand years: for a thousand years it was riotous heady mead, it was wine in the veins of warriors – and to this hour it is laughter in the heart of the hills.

HOW THE GUBBAUN SAOR WENT INTO THE COUNTRY OF THE EVER-YOUNG

Not a wind stirred.

The Son of the Gubbaun Saor leaned his elbows on a grey wave-worn rock, and his face on his hands.

The sea lay basking on a slant of ivory sand, spreading and stretching itself like a huge dragon that feels the sun; drawing long breaths, lazily conscious of its own bulk and the strength it had. It was of a wonderful colour, like the sky at dawn, like a lapis-stone bathed in honey.

"Heart of my Life," cried the Son of the Gubbaun Saor, "it is not enough to be blue: if you could see the light filtering through the young leaves in a beechwood – that greenness as of fire, that motion, that pulse of colour, you would not bask so easily. Stir yourself, Heart of my Life!"

The huge bulk of the sea responded with an almost imperceptible gesture: it was as if the dragon winked, or stretched out in lazy supercilious recognition a handful of curved claws and drew them back, as a lazy, friendly cat stretches and withdraws them.

The Son of the Gubbaun Saor laughed, and as he laughed two waves ran in like dancers on tiptoe: they were like butterflies that feign to alight, but rise again fluttering upward, poising themselves, swaying rhythmically: they were light as thistledown in a wind: they were tenuous and curved and delicate like the petal of a rose – against the marvel of that blueness they were of an incredible green.

The Son of the Gubbaun Saor clapped his hands: he cried aloud: "My Love of Loves you are! My Feathered Bird you are! Bright Pulse of Flame you are! My Branch with Silver Blossoms! My One Choice!"

His eyes caressed the sea: he stretched his hands to it, but as he stood breathless with joy, a voice came faintly over the grassy sward to him, a distant voice calling him by name. He turned from the rock and saw that Aunya was coming towards him over the short grass that had so many little purple and white flowers in it, low-growing, close-woven in it. She walked as he had seen her walk on that first day when he came through the wind-swept gap suddenly on the plain with crimson blossoms. Her heavy hair was like spun gold. He thought the time long till he could change words with her. She did not speak till she was close to him.

"You must hasten back," she said; "the House-Father has need of us both."

"Is it a blossoming of luck, or misfortune?" asked the Son.

"I know not," she said. "He slept through the sunrise, he slept through the bright whiteness of the day: 'tis but a little while since he wakened with a great cry – a vision, a portent from beyond the world had come to him: he would have us both together for the telling of it."

Aunya took her husband's hand: she did not need to hasten the home-coming.

The Gubbaun was seated in his carved chair. He had clothed himself as though he would speak with kings. His face was like a mask on one that is dead. He moved his hands feebly, they did not know whether in explanation or entreaty, but he did not speak.

"You had a word for us," said the Son.

"I had the Master-Word," said the Gubbaun. "I had knowledge enough to make a sky of stars. Now it is gone from me."

"You know the talk of the birds," said the Son, "and the talk of the beasts, and the talk of the grasses. Is that not enough?"

"I knew the joy that is in the heart of the sun! I knew the secret of life. Now it is gone."

He said no more. He sat day-long like a stone. He lay night-long like a stone; like a sea-crag when the water ebbs from it. For the length of time the moon takes to broaden and grow slender he was like that: strength ebbed from him.

"My thousand griefs!" cried the Son, "he will die: he will not leave behind him the wisdom of his craft!"

"Go to him," said Aunya, "when day whitens. Ask him what tree is king of the forest. It may be that the brightness of his mind will come back to him: if it comes back, cry out that the Dune of Angus is fallen!"

The Son of the Gubbaun rose early. He kindled a fire with boughs of the blackthorn. He dipped the palms of his hands in clear cold well-water. He wrapped himself in a cloak the colour of an amethyst stone.

He went and stood before the Gubbaun.

"O Wonder-Smith, O Master-Builder," he cried, *"The Sun is mirrored in the Sacred Well.* What Tree is King of the Forest?"

"I know a Forest," said the Gubbaun, "the roots of it go down deep, deep into the heart of the earth: the branches of it spread among the stars: the stars are fruit upon its branches. The leaves of it make a singing in my mind – singing and sleep."

The Son came forth from the chamber. "His mind is tangled in dreams," he said.

"Go to him," said Aunya, "when tomorrow whitens."

The Son of the Gubbaun rose early. He kindled a fire with boughs of the yew. He dipped the palms of his hands in clear cold well-water. He wrapped himself in a cloak the colour of embers.

He went and stood before the Gubbaun.

"O Wonder-Smith, O Master-Builder," he cried, *"The Moon moves whitely in the Sacred Wood.* What Tree is King of the Forest?"

"I know a Forest," said the Gubbaun, "a dark Forest – the leaves of it are days and years, the twisted boughs of it are centuries and millenniums – and I am tangled in its dark and crooked ways: I am caught in its thorny branches: I am lost."

The Son came forth from the chamber. "His mind is tangled in dreams," he said.

"Go to him," said Aunya, "at the whitening of to-morrow.

The Son of the Gubbaun rose early. He kindled a fire with boughs of the hazel. He dipped the palms of his hands in clear cold well-water. He wrapped himself in a cloak that was spun from threads of white silver and wrought upon with red gold.

He went and stood before the Gubbaun.

"O Wonder-Smith, O Master-builder," he said, *"The Sun beholds his image in the Moon.* What Tree is King of the Forest?"

The Gubbaun opened his eyes and looked steadily at him.

"Son," he said, "that is soon told. The King of the Forest Trees is the wise gentle Holly."

The Son knew that but a moment remained in which to surprise the secret of his father's craft. He beat his hands together, he beat his forehead, he cried aloud in a voice of lamentation: "Ochone, Ochone, for the Dune of Angus: it is fallen – fallen!"

The Gubbaun raised himself on the bed.

"The Dune of Angus has not fallen," he said, "I built it: it could not fall. It has the strength of rocks. It has the strength of adamant. Storm cannot shake it. It will blunt the teeth of gnawing centuries."

"Tell your Son, O Master-Builder, how you built it. How did you lay the stones of it together?"

"I built it," said the Gubbaun, *"with a caid on a caid, a caid over a caid, and a caid between two caids. The Dune of Angus stands!"*

"It stands," cried the Son.

The Gubbaun fell back upon the bed, his face was the colour of wax.

"Son," he said, "make a music for me: my hands are done with labour."

The Son of the Gubbaun took up his flute. He played a music from the Faery Hills. Thin and faint at first and of an unearthly sweetness it filled the mind as with a heaven of stars. It had the sound of every instrument and the sound of singing voices in it. Slow rhythms moved through it like sea-waves: light, fierce rhythms leaped like flame: it turned and twisted on itself in intricate mazes and dances of delight. It rose and swelled till it filled the tent of the sky. It slid away into hollows and secret caverns of the earth – chilled and drenched with sweetness. It ebbed and ebbed, withdrawing itself as Cleena's Wave withdraws – a ripple of foam on the void – an echo – a soundless abysm.

The Son of the Gubbaun Saor laid down his flute. No one spoke: but a sudden wind shook the house, and on it there drifted out of a clear sky, petals of snow – white as blossoms shaken from the Silver Branch.

The Gubbaun Saor was dead.

POEMS FROM

THE ROSE OF HEAVEN
(1920) AND

TO THE LITTLE
PRINCESS: AN EPISTLE
(1930)

In these poems, stretching over a period of ten years, Ella Young can be seen to be refining her work and looking towards the East as well as the Celtic world for inspiration. In the first two poems we see Ella exploring the multifaceted world of myth and legend where the questing of the heart merges with the sacred search for the divine. In "To The Little Princess," written shortly after arriving in America, Ella honours her long friendship with W.B. Yeats' muse, Maud Gonne. Herself a living legend, Gonne was also referred to by Ella as the High King's Daughter – the personification of the sacred aspect of the Irish land.

THE ROSE OF HEAVEN

I had for heritage a sword
And a rich cloak of cramoisie;
I gave them both away to you
With the good hound that followed me.

You took the cloak between your hands
And broidered on the silken hem
Strange beasts and flowers and golden stars:
It was great joy to look at them.

You graved a rune upon the sword;
You kissed the hound between the eyes;
You said, "Take back your gifts again,
Keep tryst with me in Paradise."

Beyond the four seas of the world
The high, white hills of Heaven are,
And who so seeks them sees no more
The sun or moon or any star.

The hours are like a stooping hawk,
The days are like a flight of swans,
But long, and long, and long's the road
That brings me where my true love wonnes.

The hours go by like foot-chained thralls;
The days grope, blinded, for the sun,
And nowhere on earth's farthest verge
May tidings of that land be won.

I journey with the restless dead,
But find no road by garth or bawn,
When lo, the Grail-Knights haught and pure
Pass in the stillness of the dawn.

I see the rune that my sword has,
Graved on their sword-blades broad and bare:
Their horses all are ghostly white,
The night-dew clings about their hair.

"Comrade of the Sword," they cry,
"To the far Hills of Heaven we ride;
Take horse and amour for your need
And cast your silken cloak aside."

"O fain were I of helm and steed,
But of my cloak I am more fain."
They shake their reins and ride away:
No one of them looks back again.

The Plains of Heaven change and glow
Star-sown with flowers of living flame:
When you walk there at eventide
Some day you'll hear me call your name.

The road is long, the shadows pass,
But shade and shine to me are one:
In the still fields of Paradise
My ladye sees nor moon nor sun.

"Now whither bound, Sir Wayfarer?"
A glad voice calls, I turn and see
A noble company of youths
With hounds like my hound, leashed and free.

"We go to rouse a gold-horned stag
In the wide Plains of Heaven to-day;
Bring your good hound to hunt with ours
And throw your heavy sword away."

"I had my sword from my ladye,
And I will keep it as she bade."
Without ado they turn aside
Like friends to whom farewell is said.

A young wood hides them as they go
Like the spring winds upon their way:
The milk-white Stag of Paradise
Will leap before the hounds to-day.

The Towers of Heaven builded high
Know all the proud angelic faces:
Azrael is their sentinel
And for their ward Ithuriel paces.

My ladye looks at morn and eve
Over the wall of chrysoprase:
She is full fain that I should be
Assoiled of earth and grievous days.

Full fain am I to be assoiled
If I might well such guerdon win,
But whoso seeks the Towers of Heaven
Seeks long ere he may enter in.

Sometimes the night draws on apace
Filled with strange shapes of doom and fret,
They press and clutch me as I go:
The darkness takes me in a net.

Then ruddy as the rising sun
Light flashes from a mansion fair;
Full joyous are the guests within
And the great Lords of Song are there!

They smile and call me: "Enter in,
Dear Brother of the Broidered Cloak,
Leave your fierce hound, and feast with us
For here be many of your folk."

"The hound I have has followed me
Since last I saw my ladye's face,
And for the sake of feast and song
I will not leave him in this place."

They turn their haughty eyes away;
A sudden music mounts and swells,
And through the dark I journey on
To that House where my ladye dwells.

The apple-trees of Paradise
Stretch blossomed boughs beyond the stars
Their leaves are all of silver bright
And no rough wind a blossom mars.

Mayhap I shall be old and worn,
All-spent before I come to you,
And in the garth of Paradise
I will not seem the man you knew.

But I will show the Cloak and say:
"Look, it has still its broidered gold,
And I have brought again the Sword
That once your own two hands did hold."

[The following verses were added in Ella Young's 1938 collection Marzilian. *We include them here as an indication of her continuing revision of her work]*

Then you will know me, knowing well
The Sword, the Cloak, the noble Hound,
And greet me as right-welcome guest
On Paradisal ground.

You'll pluck for me an apple down
From the heaven-branching tree,
And tasting it I'll win to youth
And all that world's felicity.

THE SAN-GRAIL

Sir Lancelot rode between the trees,
The evening sun was red:
He thought upon Queen Guinevere
With hair outspread.

He thought upon the Holy Grail
That he had come to win,
And knew his love of Guinevere
Was deadly sin.

Then from his horse he lighted down
Beneath the treen
And prayed that God would sain his soul
Of Arthur's queen.

A sudden glory filled the wood,
And there his eyes
Beheld a wonder that had come
From Paradise.

He saw the Grail-Maid with the Grail
Between her hands,
The sight that is most beautiful
In the world's lands.

Full humbly Lancelot bowed himself
Shamed and afraid
But the Grail-Maiden said to him
"Be not dismayed."

"Look up," she said, "and see the Grail
If thine eyes endure
And if thy heart hath flame of love
Through Love made pure."

He lifted up his eyes if so
The San-Grail might be found:
The splendour smote him to the earth
Deep in a swound.

But through the swound Sir Lancelot knew
The Grail-Maid stood
Like a bright-coloured bird of Heaven
In a dark wood.

And he besought of Christ the Lord
To lend him grace,
Although he might not see the Grail
To see her face.

"Look up," she said," and see my face,
The grace is won:
Quenched in me now the moon-fire is
And the fire of the sun."

He looked upon the Grail-Maid's face
Enshadowed by her hair:
He knew her, wan, and white, and still,
Queen Guinevere!

Ella Young, in her Garden, Oceano, California, 1949.
Photograph by Clara E. Sipprell.

FROM: TO THE LITTLE PRINCESS: AN EPISTLE
(1930)

THE SILVER MASK

While all the world is dusk and chill
Shaken and wan and vigourless
Because the sun-hawk takes his rest
And none to waken him may dare
Though wild swans trumpet clangorously
Stirring the cold and slumberous air
Through the white dawn I'll ride, Princess
Your page upon a high emprise
Your page in lover's tales most wise
And chivalrous pacts conned from a book
Which now he shelters in his breast
Riding alone on a perilous quest
From a city on a hill:
A city walled about with towers
Where languorous banners droop like flowers
Asleep because the wind is still.

Clattering down the cobbled street
By minaret and balcony
By turret and dark postern gate
(Fire scattering from my horse's feet)
I'll ride into the morn, elate.
Shrilly my white war-horse will neigh,
For by me crowned with rose and bay
And odorous small buds of May
A joyous company will ride,
(Their horse's hoof-beats echoless
Lords that no dream can now distress
Though helmed and crowned for sake thereof)
The flower and flame of chivalry
The lords and paladins of Love:
(And yet their brows keep asphodel.)
Jongleurs they are and errant knights
Haught paladins of olden time

Lovers that live in lovely rhyme
With faces rapt and the eyes a-gleam
Wrought in the fabric of a dream
The Lords Gawain and Palodeme
Amis and Bors from Camelot
With Lords from Ys and Inisfail,
Perador that sought the Grail
In paynim lands, and Lancelot
Who lost it for a strand of hair
Loosed on the cheek of Guinevere:
Tristagil that no sword could tame,
Trostan that kept his tryst of love
Alien in the Country of the Dead
And found between the woven boughs
Where Chimaeras and Gryphons house
His ladye beautiful like flame
And clasped and kissed her golden head:
Yvan who heard Daureenya's song
In the deep-lilied hidden solitude:
Merlin who in the thorn-branched wood
Where Vivian is, felt death no wrong
A-drowse in her pleasaunce to brood
Her dusk pleasaunce where sleep is good
Where sleep and song together go
(Such pale sweet light her beauty shed)
Where drowsy sleep-charmed lilies grow
And pomegranates ruby red
And strange proud fruits no heart can know.

Companioned thus with dream I'll ride
No mortal else astir but I,
One star yet burning in the sky
Amid wind shaken cypress trees:
(Dolorous sombre cypress trees
Dusk and tall and spired like flame.)
Flickering the shadows lie
Flickering white moths go by;
Scarlet blossoms in the grass
Sway and tremble as I pass
And sleepy songbirds flute your name.

THE MASK OF GOLD

Like a pearl your palace lies
Slumber sealing up its eyes
Deep as the peace of Paradise:
Light airs about it soft and cool,
One star trembling in the skies
One star in the lilied pool.

No sleepy lotus-buds unclose
Dream-heavy is the rose
The shadowed lawn is bare:
Unstirred by flute or shawm
The honeyed air
Dreams with no petal shed,
Dreams till the dawn-star dies from out his place
Till the swart sun uprears his face
The Archer of the Skies,
Till like a stricken fawn
The dappled twilight flies,
Then like lilies
Slender and tall
Come your maidens,
Singing all:

"Petal of poppy red
Wind-blown
Wind sped,
Cloud-shadow on the thorn:
So light, so frail is morn,
So lightly shed.

Morn is a petal blown
From the Rose of Day
Like airy thistledown
It floats away.

Frailer than buds of sorrel
That grow 'neath thorn and laurel
Is morn, and fair

Like a rose that dies
With scarce its chalice shown.

Lady arise, arise,
Unclose your lotus eyes
Ere morn be flown."

But from the pillows of your bed
You will not lift your head
Till with trumpets softly blown
Music for your ear alone
Comes a page with drooping sheaf
Of dew-wet roses thorn and leaf,
Comes a herald page to say:
"Rose-Ladye, it is day
Little winds in play
Chase the shadows here and there
Moth-wings fly away
Spindle-blossoms shake
Dew-cobwebs from their hair.
Ladye, your page would dare
Entreat you to wake
And with the rose the message take:

    Ladye most noble I bring
    A message from the King
    Your Royal father the High King:
    For you, Princess, he waits
    In the rose-garth by the Dragon Gates,
    And honeyed to the brim
    Golden morning waits with him.

Unclose your lotus-eyes
Arise, arise."

Then you will clap your hands and cry:
"Come haste, come haste, my tire-woman,
There is none so late a-bed as I:
Come haste, come haste, the moments fly:
Chaste, my tire-woman."

First will come a damsel small
With the pierced pomander-ball
Sovereign to ward off maladies:
Then girls with unguents heavy-sweet
With balm of myrrh and rosemary
With cassia buds and sendal spice,
Lithe girls on lissom feet:
They'll bring you robes of Tyrian dye
And dull red samite pranked with gems,
Robes whose broidered hems
Are thick with rose and jasmine stems
And broidered flowers of columbine.
(Hasten! Hasten! For the golden day
The gold dust moments slip away
Haste all my laggard tire-women!")
They'll bring you combs of bone and jade
Mirrors inlaid with lazuli
And Turkis-stone from Samarkand,
Prisoning with so light a hand
Your tresses in a silver net
With rubies and pale emeralds set.
(And still you'll bid them haste.)
They'll bring you heavy hoods of vair
They'll bring you cloaks of minaver
Bind on your feet the sandaled shoon,
(Your flower-fair feet so soon, so soon
In the rose-garth to be.)

Your father, I, beside the Dragon Gates
To sit unvexed and wait
Old and content and wise
With down-bent head and half-shut eyes
And drowsy thoughts that stray
To long-gone hours – or yesterday.
So I shall dream in the sun
Of years that backward run
And look upon your face
Smiling or sad
Ere the best haste you had
Could reach this place:

To see you like silver rain
A light-foot child again
Dancing beneath the almond trees,
The newly blossomed almond trees
In a lawn with daisies pied
The wind and you naught beside.

Or see you maiden-grown
And heart-bewildered by the stress
Of your own loveliness
Lovely as the moon half shown
In twilight skies alone.

Or when Spring is met
With dance and song
And priests bear forth the rood
From the high altar where 'tis set
See you in the strait cypress wood
With Blanchelys and Amoret
And other ladies gay of mood
Weaving a chaplet for your head
Rosen and lily white and red,
Or wandering sorrowful and lone
For sake of cities overthrown
Lost argosies and drownéd kings:
Yourself more cold than Dian queen
Slow pacing on the charméd green
Beneath the Oaks of Thessaly,
Or like a naiad whose wet hair
Keeps the sea-foam tangled there,
Or a sudden singing bird of the air!

So with mocking elfish grace
In that rose-enchanted place
Tryst of dream you'll keep with me
Lingering sale airily
The while the trumps of morning blow
To pleasure you, most sweet and low
And lily pale your maidens stand
With combs of jade and ivory
And Turkis-stone from Samarkand.

THE MASK TOOTHED WITH JACINTH

When high of heart
The lavish sun
Squanders his gold
In every dusty mart
I'll be a Tyrrhenian merchantman
With golden ear-rings and swart face
And a beaked ship from some far place:
Cordoba or Ispahan.
Rubies I'll have for which the Kahn
Bartered cities in Cathay
And strings of pearls from Khorassan
With rare strange birds and fruited trees
Spice-trees that hold the air a-swoon
Pallidly fragrant at high noon
Long-voyaged, hoarded, sacred trees
Whose images in stone are spread
Desolate in Carchemish.
Such trees in Babylon of old
Leaned upon terraced ways of gold
And bearded kings sat in their shade.
Such trees as these her captains brought
The subtle-sweet Egyptian queen
Such incense-dropping trees she set
Where Anthony and she had met
Beside the banks of the Nilus stream.

And cups I'll have she might have held
Between her hands at feasts she made,
Cups of chalcedony and jade
Bowls of carved sard and chrysolite.
Rare bowls of lapis I'll have too
And beads of turquoise green and blue
Ivories pierced to win delight
Peacocks than lotus-buds more white
Silks of the reddest Tyrian dyes
Indian gods with ruby eyes
Apes and birds-of-paradise.

Bronzed by such outlandish sun
Rumour of me will run
Until it reaches you, Princess,
Late or soon.
Then some high noon
Some blazoned day
Trumpeters will come my way
Summoning my ship
Commanding me
The Royal Princess deigns to see
My far-brought merchandise.

Gold and Vermilion my ship
Leans against the wharf's black lip
(The sea beyond burns lapis blue
And Turkis-green and emerald sheer)
Today you come aboard,
Gold cloths are spread for you
And cloths of red:
The high noon sun is lit
To guide you here
To gild your head
With young lords debonair
With all your lily maids to stare
At my rich hoard and ransack it.

Nubian slaves pile up the store
A gorgeous spilth, and search for more
Their bare feet pattering eagerly:
Sickle sharp against the sky
The light sea-swallows wheel and cry,
Watching their flight you'll talk with me
Of wonders and the sea.

I'll tell you of white water-sprites
That dance the waves on moonlit nights
Making music for the Sea-Kings daughters
Of thunder-dragons and of skies
Where three suns float bubble-wise
Fringed and aurioled

But cold, cold –
And how when a mariner has wandered long
Long, and overlong on the waters
Suddenly the Tower of Sardonyx
Rises ebon-black from the sea
Where the frost bites bitterly
Far, very far in the North.
The sea breaks there
Stark-toothed.
Breaks with laughter and tears
A sound that is doom in the ears
Like the witch-queen's song,
For there long since with a song she drew
With a single glittering thread of hair
Behemoth the hot seas knew
Orcus and tusked narwhales
Dragons with emerald scales
Blind dragons without eyes
And fishes pied with rose and blue
Finned fish like butterflies.

Within the Tower a music sighs
And mocks the waves and dies:
The sea-witch there alone
On a carved and gilded throne
Sits singing with her long bright hair
Sits weaving thread by thread
Red-gold from the heavy locks of her head
A pall for her lover, dead
These thousand years.

I'll tell you of a city wan
And hoar with age, and desert now
The city of King Suleiman,
At its gates stone Genii bow
Motionless hour by hour:
A temple like a scarlet flower
Blossoms in that eyeless place
Shining to the air it springs
Its pinnacles have life, it sings,

It sings,
It sings in the city of Suleiman
Empty now and desert wan.
There the sun and wind may trace
Crine of bull, or demon-face,
Djinns, Afreets, and warring Kings,
Cherubim with spread of wings
Terrible to behold.

Never mortal foot may win
To the sanctuary within
Lazuli and gold
There neath a dome of chrysoprase
Curved like a wave with sculptured swirl
Of deva, god, and dancing girl,
Where sunlight drowning splendour sheds
Three hooded serpents raise their heads:
Their hooded heads are plumed with flame,
Deep deep from the Abyss they came
Swaying to an unsung tune
Flecked and freaked with sun and moon
Huge huge from the Abyss.

Above a crystal stone
They sway and make great moan:
Plumed and scaled with fire
They sway and never tire –
But you will tire and turn away
Nor think of me beyond a day.

THE MASK OF WHITE JADE

When quiet takes the westering sun
Like a great gold-fish in her net:
And you're half sorry day is done
Yet would not have the huntress stayed,
I'll be a little broidering-maid
Among the others, skilled to make

89

Buds and blossoms for your sake
On robes of samite lined with vair.
I'll sit at my embroidery-frame
With nimble fingers and bent head
Working with pearl and cramoisy
On cloth of gold and silver thread:
And heedless of the talk that goes
From girl to girl like wind that blows
The heads of flowering grass together
I'll dream of sorrowful proud things
That are like you, till evening brings
Yourself with all the courtly train
Who follow you, and once again
You stop to praise the hoods of vair
And samite with their flowers a-stare.

Your voice will waken memories
Of some far off enchanted place
Of some long perished loveliness
Pale as the pale rose of your face:
The heavy splendour of your hair
Will snare and mind me tress by tress,
The sorcery of the weariness
That weighs your heavy-lidded eyes
And weighs your hands and ways your feet
As flowers are weighed upon by rain
Will weigh upon me, half a pain
And half a rapture unaware
Of anything in earth or air,
Till wondering at you I surmise
Some Lord of Faery made you wise
In all the wizard arts he knew
Before the Eden apple grew.

The trumpets blown at eventide
Will sound far off and strange and sweet
Like voices calling in a dream:
And you will pass when day is done,
With the slow lingering vermeil sun,
Like a haught dream that lifts and sways

90

The beauty of the world, and lays
A rapturous sorrow on the heart.

Silence and dusk when you are gone
Will spread a sudden ghostly peace
On all things and bid sorrow cease
For quiet takes the westering sun.

THE MASK WITH CLOSED LIDS

When the sun's lost and all the light
That followed him is drowned in night
You'll climb a little secret stair
That leads into a turret room
Where half in light and half in gloom
On every wall the arras gay
Keeps a perpetual holiday
Of fauns and dryads in a wood.
The wind outside will croon and sigh
And dusk-hued things will wander by
Brushing the darkness with their wings:
But when you come into the room
Tall candles will be lighted there.

You'll sit in a great carven chair
With your hands idle in your lap
And I'll be with you. I shall be
A little child beside your knee
And you will tell me faery tales
Or read them to me from a book
Into which I scarce dare look
Because it's full of spells and charms
And painted kings and men-at-arms
And flowers that border every page.
You'll read me tales of Joyous Garde
And the Land Under Wave, unmarred
By any breath of heaviness:
And while you read to me I know

The wind will stir the candle flame
And move the arras to and fro
and I'll cry to you: "Let us go
To Broceliande beyond the sea
And lose ourselves there endlessly:
There no one counts the passing hours
There pards and unicorns are seen
Led in a leash by a pale queen
Who stays to gather starry flowers:
Could we not go with the light foot-fall
Where the white deer go slim and tall
Where birds with honeyed voices call
And golden apples merrily
Swing up and down on every tree?
Let us sail and sail away
All the night and all the day
Sail, and seek that forest old
In a boat that will not hold
Anyone but you and me."

Then you will smile or maybe sigh
And say: "Dear heart, we'll find the boat
Step into it and be a-float
On that still sea whose colour vies
With all the gems of Paradise."

And I'll believe you and be glad,
So glad that I must shut my eyes
And lean my face against your hand,
And so I'll sleep, and over me
Will flow the radiance of the sea
That touches the Enchanted Land.

CELTIC WONDER TALES
(1910)

In these stories we are in the hands of a master writing at the height of her powers. Though one of her earliest collections, this has proved one of the most popular with dozens of reprints over the years. Turning to her first love, Irish mythology, and especially the great epic tales of the gods, Ella Young weaves an extraordinary spell over her readers. In the first story, 'The Earthly Shapers', we have what is virtually a creation myth (something missing from Celtic myth in general), while in 'The Eric Fine of Lugh' we see explored the intricate idea of a fine levied against all who cause hardship or death to others, and from which even gods are not exempt.

THE EARTHLY SHAPERS

In Tir-na-Moe, the Land of the Living Heart, Brigit was singing. Angus the Ever-Young, and Midyr the Red-Maned, and Ogma that is called Splendour of the Sun, and the Dagda and other lords of the people of Dana drew near to listen.
Brigit sang:

Now comes the hour foretold, a god-gift bringing
        A wonder-sight.
Is it a star new-born and splendid up springing
        Out of the night?
Is it a wave from the Fountain of Beauty up flinging
        Foam of delight?
Is it a glorious immortal bird that is winging
        Hither its flight?

It is a wave, high-crested, melodious, triumphant,
        Breaking in light.

It is a star, rose-hearted and joyous, a splendour
    Risen from night.
It is flame from the world of the gods, and love runs before it,
    A quenchless delight.

Let the wave break, let the star-rise, let the flame leap.
Ours, if our hearts are wise,
    To take and keep.

Brigit ceased to sing, and there was silence for a little space in Tir-na-Moe. Then Angus said:

"Strange are the words of your song, and strange the music: it swept me down steeps of air – down – down – always further down. Tir-na-Moe was like a dream half-remembered. I felt the breath of strange worlds on my face, and always your song grew louder and louder, but you were not singing it. Who was singing it?"

"The Earth was singing it."

"The Earth!" said the Dagda. "Is not the Earth in the pit of chaos? Who has ever looked into that pit or stayed to listen where there is neither silence nor song?"

"O Shepherd of the Star-Flocks, I have stayed to listen. I have shuddered in the darkness that is round the Earth. I have seen the black hissing waters and the monsters that devour each other – I have looked into the groping writhing adder-pit of hell."

The light that pulsed about the De Danaan lords grew troubled at the thought of that pit, and they cried out: "Tell us no more about the Earth, O Flame of the Two Eternities, and let the thought of it slip from yourself as a dream slips from the memory."

"O Silver Branches that no Sorrow has Shaken," said Brigit, "hear one thing more! The Earth wails all night because it has dreamed of beauty."

"What dream, O Brigit?"

"The Earth has dreamed of the white stillness of dawn; of the star that goes before the sunrise; and of music like the music of my song."

"O Morning Star," said Angus, "would I had never heard your song, for now I cannot shake the thought of the Earth from me!"

"Why should you shake the thought from you, Angus the Subtle-Hearted? You have wrapped yourself in all the colours of the sunlight; are you not fain to look into the darkness and listen to the thunder of abysmal waves; are you not fain to make gladness in the Abyss?"

Angus did not answer: he reached out his hand and gathered a blossom from a branch: he blew upon the blossom and tossed it into the air: it became a wonderful white bird and circled about him singing.

Midyir the Haughty rose and shook out the bright tresses of his hair till he was clothed with radiance as with a Golden Fleece.

"I am fain to look into the darkness," he said. "I am fain to hear the thunder of the Abyss."

"Then come with me," said Brigit, "I am going to put my mantle round the Earth because it has dreamed of beauty."

"I will make clear a place for your mantle," said Midyir. "I will throw fire amongst the monsters."

"I will go with you too," said the Dagda, who is called the Green Harper.

"And I," said Splendour of the Sun, whose other name is Ogma the Wise. "And I," said Nuada Wielder of the White Light. "And I," said Gobniu the Wonder-Smith, "we will re-make the Earth!"

"Good luck to the adventure!" said Angus. "I would go myself if ye had the Sword of Light with you."

"We will take the Sword of Light," said Brigit, "and the Cauldron of Plenty and the Spear of Victory and the Stone of Destiny with us, for we will build power and wisdom and beauty and lavish-heartedness into the Earth."

"It is well said," cried all the Shining Ones. "We will take the Four Jewels."

Ogma brought the Sword of Light from Findrias the cloud-fair city that is in the east of the De Danaan world; Nuada brought the Spear of Victory from Gorias the flame-bright city that is in the south of the De Danaan world; the Dagda brought the Cauldron of Plenty from Murias the city that is builded in the west of the De Danaan world and has the stillness of deep waters; Midyir brought the Stone of Destiny from Falias the city that is builded in the north of the De Danaan world and has the steadfastness of adamant. Then Brigit and her companions set forth.

They fell like a rain of stars till they came to the blackness that surrounded the Earth, and looking down saw below them, as at the bottom of an abyss, the writhing, contorted, hideous life that swarmed and groped and devoured itself ceaselessly.

From the seething turmoil of that abyss all the Shining Ones drew back save Midyir. He grasped the Fiery Spear and descended like a flame.

His comrades looked down and saw him treading out the monstrous life as men tread grapes in a wine-press; they saw the blood and foam of that destruction rise about Midyir till he was crimson with it even to the crown of his head; they saw him whirl the Spear till it became a wheel of fire and shot out sparks and tongues of flame; they saw the flame lick the darkness and turn back on itself and spread and blossom murk-red – blood-red – rose-red at last!

Midyir drew himself out of the abyss, a Ruby Splendour, and said: "I have made a place for Brigit's mantle. Throw down your mantle, Brigit, and bless the Earth!"

Brigit threw down her mantle and when it touched the Earth it spread itself, unrolling like silver flame. It took possession of the place Midyir had made as the sea takes possession, and it continued to spread itself because everything that was foul drew back from the little silver flame at the edge of it.

It is likely it would have spread itself over all the earth, only Angus, the youngest of the gods, had not patience to wait: he leaped down and stood with his two feet on the mantle. It ceased to be fire and became a silver mist about him. He ran through the mist laughing and calling on the others to follow. His laughter drew them and they followed. The drifting silver mist closed over them and round them, and through it they saw each other like images in a dream – changed and fantastic. They laughed when they saw each other. The Dagda thrust both his hands into the Cauldron of Plenty.

"O Cauldron," he said, "you give to every one the gift that is meetest, give me now a gift meet for the Earth."

He drew forth his hands full of green fire and he scattered the greenness everywhere as a sower scatters seed. Angus stooped and lifted the greenness of the earth: he scooped hollows in it; he piled it in heaps; he played with it as a child plays with sand, and when it slipped through his fingers it changed colour and shone like star-dust, blue and purple and yellow and white and red.

Now, while the Dagda sowed emerald fire and Angus played with it, Mananaun was aware that the exiled monstrous life had lifted itself and was looking over the edge of Brigit's mantle. He saw the iron eyes of strange creatures jeering in the blackness and he drew the Sword of Light from its scabbard and advanced its gleaming edge against that chaos. The strange life fled in hissing spume, but the sea rose to greet the Sword in a great foaming thunderous wave.

Mananaun swung the Sword a second time, and the sea rose again in a wave that was green as a chrysolite, murmurous, sweet-sounding, flecked at the edges with amethyst and purple and blue-white foam.

A third time Mananaun swung the Sword, and the sea rose to greet it in a wave white as crystal, unbroken, continuous, silent as dawn.

The slow wave fell back into the sea, and Brigit lifted her mantle like a silver mist. The De Danaans saw everything clearly. They saw that they were in an island covered with green grass and full of heights and strange scooped-out hollows and winding ways. They saw too that the grass was full of flowers – blue and purple and yellow and white and red.

"Let us stay here," they said to each other, "and make beautiful things so that the Earth may be glad."

Brigit took the Stone of Destiny in her hands: it shone white like a crystal between her hands.

"I will lay the Stone in this place," she said, "that ye may have empire."

She laid the Stone on the green grass and it sank into the earth: a music rose about it as it sank, and suddenly all the scooped-out hollows and deep winding ways were filled with water – rivers of water that leaped and shone; lakes and deep pools of water trembling into stillness.

"It is the laughter of the Earth!" said Ogma the Wise.

Angus dipped his fingers in the water.

"I would like to see the blue and silver fishes that swim in Connla's Well swimming here," he said, "and trees growing in this land like those trees with blossomed branches that grow in the Land of the Silver Fleece."

"It is an idle wish, Angus the Young," said Ogma. "The fishes in Connla's Well are too bright for these waters and the blossoms that grow on silver branches would wither here. We must wait and learn the secret of the Earth, and slowly fashion dark strange trees, and fishes that are not like the fishes in Connla's Well."

"Yea," said Nuada, "we will fashion other trees, and under their branches shall go hounds that are not like the hound Failinis and deer that have not horns of gold. We will make ourselves the smiths and artificers of the world and beat the strange life out yonder into other shapes. We will make for ourselves islands to the north of this and islands to the west, and round them shall go also the three waves of Mananaun for we will fashion and re-fashion all things till there is nothing unbeautiful left in the whole earth."

"It is good work," cried all the De Danaans, "We will stay and do it, but Brigit must go to Moy Mell and Tir-na-Moe and Tir-nan-Oge and Tir-fo-Tonn, and all the other worlds, for she is the Flame of Delight in every one of them."

"Yes, I must go," said Brigit.

"O Brigit!" said Ogma, "Before you go, tie a knot of remembrance in the fringe of your mantle so that you may always remember this place – and tell us, too, by what name we shall call this place."

"Ye shall call it the White Island," said Brigit, "and its other name shall be the Island of Destiny; and its other name shall be Ireland."

Then Ogma tied a knot of remembrance in the fringe of Brigit's mantle.

THE SPEAR OF VICTORY

Nuada, Wielder of the White Light, set up the Spear of Victory in the centre of Ireland. It was like a great fiery fountain. It was like a singing flame. It burned continually, and from it every fire in Ireland was kindled. The glow of it reached up to the mountain tops. The glow of it reached under the forest trees. The glow of it shot into the darkness and made a halo of light far beyond the three waves of Mananaun. The mis-shapen things of the darkness came to the edge of the halo. They sunned themselves in it; they got strength from it. They began to build a habitation for themselves in the dark waters. They took shapes to themselves, and dark cunning wisdom. Balor the One-Eyed was their king. They were minded to get the Spear of Victory.

They compassed Ireland. They made a harsh screeching. The De Danaans said to each other:

"It is only the Fomor, the people from under the sea, who are screeching; they will tire of it!"

They did not tire of it: they kept up the screeching. The De Danaans tired of it. Nuada took up the Spear of Victory. He whirled it. He threw it into the blackness that it might destroy the Fomor. It went through them like lightning through storm-clouds. It made a great destruction. Balor grasped it. He had the grip! The Spear stayed with him. It was like a fiery serpent twisting every way. He brought it into his own country. There was a lake in the middle of his own country full of black water. Whoever tasted that water would forget anything he knew. Balor put the fiery head of the Spear in that lake. It became a column of red-hot iron. He could not draw it out of the lake.

The Spear was in the lake then. Great clouds of steam rose about it from the black water. Out of the hissing steam Demons of the Air were born. The Demons were great and terrible. There was an icy wind about them. They found their way into Ireland. They took prey there in spite of the De Danaans. They made broad tracks for themselves. The Fomor followed in their tracks. It was then that misfortune came to the De Danaans. The people of the Fomor got the better of the De Danaans. They took the Cauldron of Plenty and the Magic Harp from the Dagda. They made themselves lords and hard rulers over the De Danaans, and they laid Ireland under tribute. They were taking tribute out of it ever and again till Lugh Lauve Fauda came. 'Twas he that broke the power of the Fomor and sent the three sons of Dana for the Spear. They had power to draw it out of the lake. They gave it to Lugh, and it is with him it is now, and 'tis he will set it up again in the middle of Ireland before the end of the world.

THE COMING OF LUGH

Mananaun mac Lir, who rules the ocean, took the little Sun-God, Lugh, in his arms and held him up so that he could see the whole of Ireland with the waves whispering about it everywhere.

"Say farewell to the mountains and rivers, and the big trees and the flowers in the grass, O Lugh, for you are coming away with me."

The child stretched out his hands and cried: "Good-bye, mountains and flowers and rivers: some day I will come back to you."

Then Mananaun wrapped Lugh in his cloak and stepped into his boat, the Ocean-Sweeper, and without oar or sail they journeyed over the sea till they crossed the waters at the edge of the world and came to the country of Mananaun – a beautiful country shining with the colours of the dawn.

Lugh stayed in that country with Mananaun. He raced the waves along the strand; he gathered apples sweeter than honey from trees with crimson blossoms: and wonderful birds came to play with him. Mananaun's daughter, Niav, took him through woods where there were milk-white deer with horns of gold, and black-maned lions and spotted panthers, and unicorns that shone like silver, and strange beasts that no one ever heard of; and all the animals were glad to see him, and he played with them and called them by their names. Every day he grew taller and stronger and more beautiful, but he did not any day ask Mananaun to take him back to Ireland.

Every night when darkness had come into the sky, Mananaun wrapped himself in his mantle of power and crossed the sea and walked all round Ireland, stepping from rock to rock. No one saw him, because his mantle made him invisible, but he saw everything and knew that trouble had found the De Danaans. The ugly, mis-shapen folk of the Fomor had come into Ireland and spread themselves over the country like a pestilence.

They had stolen the Cauldron of Plenty and carried it away to their own land, where Balor of the Evil Eye reigned. They had taken the Spear of Victory also, and the only one of the four great Jewels of Sovereignty remaining to the De Danaans was the Stone of Destiny. It was hidden deep in the earth of Ireland, and because of it the Fomorians could not altogether conquer the country, nor could they destroy the De Danaans, though they drove them from their pleasant palaces and hunted them through the glens and valleys like outlaws.

Mananaun himself had the fourth Jewel, the Sword of Light: he kept it and waited.

When Lugh was full grown, Mananaun said to him: "It is three times seven years, as mortals count time, since I brought you to Tir-nan-Oge, and in all that time I have never given you a gift. To-day I will give you a gift."

He brought out the Sword of Light and gave it to Lugh, and when Lugh took it in his hand he remembered how he had cried to the hills and rivers of Ireland – "Some day I will come back to you!" And he said to Mananaun:

"I want to go back to Ireland."

"You will not find joyousness there, O Lugh, or the music of harp strings, or feasting. The De Danaans are shorn of their strength. Ogma, their Champion, carries logs to warm Fomorian hearths; Angus wanders like an outcast; and Nuada, the King, has but one dun, where those who had once the lordship of the world meet in secret like hunted folk."

"I have a good sword," said Lugh. "I will go to my kinsfolk."

"O Lugh," said Mananaun, "they have never known you. Will you leave me, and Niav, and this land where sorrow has never touched you, for the sake of stranger kinsfolk?"

Lugh answered: "I remember the hills and the woods and the rivers of Ireland, and though all my kinsfolk were gone from it and the sea covered everything but the tops of the mountains, I would go back."

"You have the hardiness that wins victory," said Mananaun. "I will set you on my own white horse and give you companions as high-hearted as yourself. I will put my helmet on your head and my breast-plate over your heart: you shall drive the Fomorians out of Ireland as chaff is driven by the wind."

When Lugh put on the helmet of Mananaun, brightness shot into the sky as if a new sun had risen; when he put on the breast-plate, a great wave of music swelled and sounded through Tir-nan-Oge; when he mounted the white horse, a mighty wind swept past him, and the companions Mananaun had promised rode beside him. Their horses were white like his, and gladness that age cannot wither shone in their faces. When they came to the sea that is about Tir-nan-Oge, the little crystal waves lifted themselves up to look at Lugh, and when he and his comrades sped over the sea as lightly as blown foam, the little waves followed them till they came to Ireland, and the Three Great Waves of Ireland thundered a welcome – the Wave of Thoth; the Wave of Rury; and the long, slow, white, foaming Wave of Cleena.

No one saw the Faery Host coming into Ireland. At the place where their horses leaped from sea to land there was a great wood of pine trees.

"Let us go into the wood," said Lugh, and they rode between the tall straight tree-trunks into the silent heart of the wood.

"Rest here," said Lugh, "till morning. I will go to the dun of Nuada and get news of my kinsfolk."

He put his shining amour from him and wrapped himself in a dark cloak and went on foot to the dun of Nuada. He struck the brazen door, and the Guardian of the Door spoke to him from within.

"What do you seek?"

"My way into the dun."

"No one enters here who has not his craft. What can you do?"

"I have the craft of a Carpenter."

"We have a carpenter within; he is Luchtae, son of Luchaid."

"I have the craft of a Smith."

"We have a smith within, Colum of the three new ways of working."

"I have the craft of a Champion."

"We have a champion within; he is Ogma himself."

"I have the craft of a Harper."

"We have a harper within, even Abhcan, son of Bicelmos; the Men of the Three Gods chose him in the faery hills."

"I have the craft of a Poet and Historian."

"We have a poet and historian within, even En, son of Ethaman."

"I have the craft of a Wizard."

"We have many wizards and magicians within."

"I have the craft of a Physician."

"We have a physician within, even Dian Cecht."

"I have the craft of a Cupbearer."

"We have nine cupbearers within."

"I have the craft of a Brazier."

"We have a brazier within, even Credne Cerd."

"Go hence and ask your king if he has within any one man who can do all these things. If he has, I will not seek to enter."

The Guardian of the Door hurried in to Nuada.

"O King," he said, "The most wonderful youth in the world is waiting outside your door to-night! He seeks admittance as the Ildana, the Master of Every Craft."

"Let him come in," said King Nuada.

Lugh came into the dun. Ogma, the Champion, took a good look at him. He thought him young and slender, and was minded to test him. He stooped and lifted the Great Stone that was before the seat of the King. It was flat and round, and four score yoke of oxen could not move it. Ogma cast it through the open door so that it crossed the fosse which was round the dun. That was his challenge to the Ildana.

"It is a good champion-cast," said Lugh. "I will better it."

He went outside. He lifted the Stone and cast it back – not through the door, but through the strong wall of the dun – so that it fell in the place where it had lain before Ogma lifted it.

"Your cast is better than mine!" said Ogma. "Sit in the seat of the champion with your face to the King."

Lugh drew his hand over the wall; it became whole as before. He sat in the champion-seat.

"Let chess be brought," said the King.

They played, and Lugh won all the games, so that thereafter it passed into a proverb "to make the Cro of Lugh."

"Truly you are the Ildana," said Nuada. "I would fain hear music of your making, but I have no harp to offer you."

"I see a kingly harp within reach of your hand," said Lugh.

"That is the harp of the Dagda. No one can bring music from that harp but himself. When he plays on it, the four Seasons – Spring, Summer, Autumn, and Winter – pass over the earth."

"I will play on it," said Lugh.

The harp was given to him.

Lugh played the music of joy, and outside the dun the birds began to sing as though it were morning and wonderful crimson flowers sprang through the grass – flowers that trembled with delight and swayed and touched each other with a delicate faery ringing as of silver bells. Inside the dun a subtle sweetness of laughter filled the hearts of every one: it seemed to them that they had never known gladness till that night.

Lugh played the music of sorrow. The wind moaned outside, and where the grass and flowers had been there was a dark sea of moving waters. The De Danaans within the dun bowed their heads on their hands and wept, and they had never wept for any grief.

Lugh played the music of peace, and outside there fell silently a strange snow. Flake by flake it settled on the earth and changed to starry dew. Flake by flake the quiet of the Land of the Silver Fleece settled in the hearts and minds of Nuada and his people: they closed their eyes and slept, each in his seat.

Lugh put the harp from him and stole out of the dun. The snow was still falling outside. It settled on his dark cloak and shone like silver scales; it settled on the thick curls of his hair and shone like jewelled fire; it filled the night about him with white radiance. He went back to his companions.

The sun had risen in the sky when the De Danaans awoke in Nuada's dun. They were light-hearted and joyous and it seemed to them that they had dreamed overnight a strange, beautiful dream.

"The Fomorians have not taken the sun out of the sky," said Nuada. "Let us go to the Hill of Usna and send to our scattered comrades that we may make a stand against our enemies."

They took their weapons and went to the Hill of Usna, and they were not long on it when a band of Fomorian devastators came upon them. The Fomorians scoffed among themselves when they saw how few the De Danaans were, and how ill-prepared for fighting.

"Behold," they cried, "what mighty kings are to-day upon Usna, the Hill of Sovereignty! Come down, O Kings, and bow yourselves before your masters! "

"We will not bow ourselves before you," said Nuada, "for ye are ugly and vile: and lords neither of us nor of Ireland."

With hoarse cries the Fomorians fell on the De Danaans, but Nuada and his folk held together and withstood them as well as they were able. Scarcely had the weapons clashed when a light appeared in the horizon and a sound of mighty battle trumpets shook the air. The light was so white that no one could look at it, and great rose-red streamers shot from it into the sky.

"It is a second sunrise!" said the Fomorians.

"It is The Deliverer!" said the De Danaans.

Out of the light came the glorious company of warriors from Tir-nan-Oge. Lugh was leading them. He had the helmet of Mananaun on his head, the breast-plate of Mananaun over his heart, and the great white horse of Mananaun beneath him.

The Sword of Light was bare in his hand. He fell on the Fomorians as a sea-eagle falls on her prey, as lightning flashes out of a clear sky. Before him and his companions they were destroyed as stubble is destroyed by fire. He held his hand when only nine of them remained alive.

"Bow yourselves," he said, "before King Nuada, and before the De Danaans, for they are your Lords and the Lords of Ireland, and go hence to Balor of the Evil Eye and tell him and his mis-shapen brood that the De Danaans have taken their own again and they will wage war against the Fomorians till there is not one left to darken the earth with his shadow."

The nine Fomorians bowed themselves before King Nuada, and before the De Danaans; and before Lugh Lauve Fauda, the Ildana; and they arose and carried his message to Balor of the Evil Eye, King of the Fomorians.

THE ERIC FINE OF LUGH

The chiefs of the Tuatha De Danaan thronged round Lugh on the Hill of Usna. Lugh stood on the summit, and the Sword of Light was bare in his hand: all the hill below him shone with a radiance like white silver.

"Chiefs," cried Lugh, "behold the Sword! Ye should have three great jewels to match it. Where are the Spear of Victory, the Cauldron of Plenty, and the Stone of Destiny?"

The Tuatha De Danaan bowed their heads and veiled their faces before Lugh, and answered: "The Fomor have taken the Cauldron of Plenty and the Spear of Victory from us. Ask the Earth of Ireland for the Stone."

Lugh whirled the Sword till it became a glancing wheel of light, and cried: "O Earth of Ireland, sacred and beloved, have you the Lia Fail, the Stone of Destiny?"

A strong sweet music welled up from the earth, and every stone and every leaf and every drop of water shone with light till all Ireland seemed one vast crystal, white and shining. The white light changed to rose, as it had been a ruby; and the ruby to sapphire; and the sapphire to emerald; the emerald to opal; the opal to amethyst; and the amethyst to diamond, white and radiant with every colour.

"It is enough!" cried Lugh. "I am well answered: the earth of Ireland has kept the Stone."

"O Chiefs," he said, "raise up your foreheads. Though ye have not the jewels ye have the scars of battle-combat, and ye have endured sorrow and hardship for ye have known what it is to be exiles in your own land. Let us swear brotherhood now by the Sword and the Stone that we may utterly destroy the Fomor and cleanse the world. Hold up your hands and swear, as I and those who came with me from Tir-nan-Oge will swear, and as the Sacred Land will swear, that we may have one mind and one heart and one desire amongst us all."

Then the De Danaans lifted up their hands and swore a great oath of brotherhood with the Earth and with the hosts of the Shining Ones from Tir-nan-Oge. They swore by the Sword of Light and the Stone of Destiny; by the Fire that is over the earth; and the Fire that is under the earth; and the Fire in the heart of heroes. They swore to have one mind, one heart, and one desire, until the Fomor should be destroyed. Lugh swore the same oath, and all his shining comrades from Tir-nan-Oge swore it. The hills and valleys and plains and rivers and lakes and forests of Ireland swore it – they all fastened the bond of brotherhood on themselves.

"Let us go hence," said Lugh, when the oath was ended, "and make ready for the great battle."

At his word all the chiefs departed, each going his own road.

Cian, the father of Lugh, was crossing the plain of Louth that is called Moy Myeerhevna: he lifted up his eyes and saw the three sons of Turann coming towards him. There was black hatred between himself and the sons of Turann, and he was minded not to meet them. He took the form of a wild boar and hid himself with a herd of swine. Brian, Ur, and Urcar, the sons of Turann, saw him do it, and anger leaped in them.

"Come forth!" they cried. "Show your face to us."

Cian did not come forth.

Ur and Urcar changed themselves into hounds and hunted the strange boar from the herd.

Brian made a cast of his spear at it, and when Cian felt the wound, he cried out: "Hold! Brian, son of Turann: do not slay me in the form of a pig!"

"Take your own form."

Cian took his own form, and said: "Ye see my face now, Sons of Turann, with blood on it. Well ye knew me from the first, and well I knew you – Oath-Breakers!"

"The bands of death on your poisonous tongue!" said Urcar. "Take back your word!"

"I will not take it back, Sons of the Adder. Slay me and every drop of blood will cry out on you – your very weapons will cry out on you in the Place of Assembly."

"We will slay you with weapons that cannot cry out," said the Sons of Turann, and they lifted great stones and rocks from the earth and stoned Cian till he was dead.

The Sons of Turann buried the body of Cian the depth of a man's height in the ground, but the earth refused to hide the body and cast it up again before them. They buried it a second time, and a second time the earth refused to hide the body and cast it up before them. Six times they buried it, and six times the earth cast it up. They buried it the seventh time, and that time the earth made no sign. The body of Cian was hidden. The Sons of Turann hastened away from the place and went to the court of King Nuada to show themselves with the other warriors.

The earth sent a little wind to Lugh Lauve Fauda. It touched his face and eyelids; it lifted the thick curls of his hair; it touched his hand as a hound touches the hand of a beloved master, and Lugh knew the wind had come for him. He followed it till he reached the place where Cian had been slain.

"O Lugh," said the earth, "the bond of brotherhood is broken. The Sons of Turann have slain your father. Look what a poor torn thing I cover!"

The Earth laid bare the body of Cian. Lugh looked at the mangled blood-stained body, and at the trampled dishonoured earth, and in his eyes two tears slowly gathered. He shook them away, and then he saw that the earth had sent up a little well of pure water close to him. He bent over it.

"O Earth," he said, "forgive the broken bond!"

The little spring in the heart of the well leaped in answer, and nine crystal bubbles rose through the water. Lugh made a cup of his two hands and lifted water from the well. He sprinkled it on the torn earth, and greenness came again to the trampled grass. He sprinkled it on the bruised body of his father, and it became whole and white again.

"O Earth," he said, "most noble and beloved, I will avenge your wrong."

"O Father," he said, "you shall yet send help for the battle, and the hands of your slayers shall bring it. 'Tis not wearisome to wait for news of victory in Moy Mell, for all the winds that blow there are winds of beauty, and now you have the crimson flowers beneath your feet and the radiance of the Silver Fleece about you."

He laid the body of Cian tenderly in the earth and went to seek the slayers at the court of King Nuada.

Nuada sat in his royal seat. There was a white light about him as it had been a fleece of silver, and round his head a wheel of light pulsed and beat with changing colours. His face was joyous and the faces of the Tuatha De Danaan were joyous. The great door of the dun was open and De Danaan chiefs came and went through it.

Lugh came into the dun and with him came such heaviness of heart that joy was shaken from the assembly.

"Why is the hero-light gone from your fore-head, O Lugh, Ildana?" said Nuada.

"It is because I have seen the dead body of my father – and the earth trampled into mire and blood."

The light went from the head of Nuada and he veiled his face. All the chiefs bowed their heads and raised the three sorrowful cries of the keene. Only the three sons of Turann remained with haughty eyes and unbowed heads.

"O Wind of Misfortune," cried the chiefs, "that brought the Fomor at the first to us!"

"It was not from the Fomor, O Chiefs, that Cian, Son of Dian-Cecht, got death – the hands that slew him have sworn the oath of brotherhood."

"Name his slayers!" cried Nuada; "and though they be our noblest and most loved – though they be even the Sons of Turann – they shall perish utterly!"

"The slayers are the three sons of Turann!"

Nuada looked on the three Sons of Turann, and when he saw they had no words to answer Lugh his heart failed him, for the three were the mightiest and most beautiful of his warriors and there was no one with more hero-gifts than Brian unless it were the Ildana himself.

"Let them perish!" said Nuada.

"Nay, King of the Tuatha De Danaan," said Lugh, "Let them make good the battle-loss! Let them pay eric for the warrior they have slain!"

"You are well named the Ildana," said the King, "for truly wisdom is with you!" and then he said to the Sons of Turann: "Will ye make good the battle-loss? Will ye pay eric for Cian, son of Dian-Cecht?"

They answered: "We will pay eric: let Lugh Lauve Fauda ask it of us."

"I ask three apples, a pig-skin, a spear, a chariot with two horses, seven swine, a hound, a cooking-spit, and three shouts on a hill."

"You have stretched out your hand for a small eric-fine, Lugh the Long-Handed."

"I have not stretched out my hand for a small fine, Brian, son of Turann. The apples I ask are three golden apples from the tree that is watched by sleepless dragons in the Eastern half of the world. The skin I ask is the skin of that pig before whom rivers of water turned into rivers of wine. The skin has power to turn whatever water it touches into wine, and if it be wrapped about a man wounded to death it will give him back his life and make his body clean and whole again. It is the jewel in a great king's treasure-house, and ye will not find it easy to get. The spear I ask is the fiery victory-giver that is kept in times of peace with its head sunk in a cauldron of magic water lest it should destroy the world. The chariot I ask is the chariot of Dobar: it outshines all chariots that have been made or shall be made. The horses yoked to it do not draw back their feet from the sea-waves: their going is as lordly on the wide plain of the sea as it is on the land. The seven pigs I ask are the pigs of Asal, the King of the Golden Pillars – though they be killed and eaten to-day, they will be alive and well to-morrow, and whoso eats of them shall never know what it is to lack strength. The hound is the hound Failinis. He is brighter than the sun at mid-summer. The beasts of the forest are astonished at the sight of him: they have no strength to contend against him. The cooking-spit is a guarded flame. Fifty-three women keep it in the island of Caer, in the green stillness that is under the sea-waves. The three shouts must be given on the hill that is guarded by Midkena and his sons — no champion since the beginning of time has raised a victory-shout on that hill. I have named my eric, sons of Turann. Do ye choose to pay it, or will ye humble yourselves and ask grace?"

"We will pay the eric," said the sons of Turann, and they went forth from the Court of King Nuada.

When the three brothers entered their father's dun they sat down in sorrow and heaviness and there was no word between them till their sister Enya came to them.

"Why does sorrow darken your faces and the faces of the household?" she asked. "What grief has come upon you?"

"We have slain Cian, son of Dian-Cecht, the father of Lugh Lauve Fauda!"

"Alas!" cried Enya, and she beat her hands together. "Alas! Ye have broken Lugh's protection out of Ireland: he will not fight in the Great Battle now!"

"Lugh will fight in the Great Battle. But he has laid on us an eric that bows us to the grave-mould."

"What eric?"

"He asks the Hound Failinis; and the Spear of Victory – he asks the Seven Treasures of the World!"

"We are undone!" said Enya. "Destruction has come upon us!"

While she spoke they heard the approaching footsteps of those who attended Turann.

"Let us go," said Urcar, "before our father sees that good days are gone from us."

"Sorrow cannot be hidden," said Enya.

Turann came into the room. He was old and his strength was withered. His sons led him to the high-seat, and when he looked on them he knew an evil thing had befallen.

"Tell me," he said, "What misfortune has come to us."

Then Brian told the story of Cian's death and what eric Lugh had bound on them. When he made an end of telling it, Turann said:

"Bitter indeed to me is the coming of the Deliverer, for he has taken from me my three sons – my Three Eagles that never failed to carry off a prey, my Three Salmon of Knowledge that could make paths for themselves in all the rivers of the world, my Three Strong Bulls that stamped on the necks of kings. It is a bitter thing to be old without my sons."

"O my Father," said Brian, "if you have bred strong sons they will set forth strongly, and it may be they will bring back the eric-spoil. Do not make a lamentation for us till we are dead!"

"Nay," said Turann, "Ye are setting forth on an adventure that knows no ending, for the treasures that ye seek are hidden in the caves of dragons and under the sea-waves. Strange kings will make a mock of you leaning over battlements of adamant and strange monsters will crush your bones. Ye will not come back to me, living or dead. No one will heap the grave-mound over your bodies!"

"O my Father," said Enya, "the heart of Lugh is set on the eric-fine. His hands are fain to grasp the fiery spear and he would see the spoils of the world brought into Ireland. Let us ask him for help. If he will give Mananaun's boat, the Ocean-Sweeper, it will not be hard for good warriors to come by the treasures – since, at a word, the Ocean-Sweeper will bear those who sit in it to whatsoever place they desire to be."

"We will ask nothing from Lugh Lauve Fauda!" said Turann's sons.

"But I will ask!" said Turann, and he cried aloud: "Let my horses be yoked and my chariot made ready! I will not sleep till I have spoken with Lugh Lauve Fauda."

When Turann came to Lugh and asked for the boat, Lugh said: "Bid your sons to make ready and set forth. When they come to the edge of the sea and their feet touch the sea-foam, Mananaun's boat will be there waiting for them."

Turann hurried home with the good answer, and his sons made ready to set forth. Their kinsfolk and the swordsmen of their father's clan went with them to the edge of the sea and when their feet touched the sea-foam they saw a little boat, such as might fit one person, waiting for them.

"Lugh has deceived us!" cried Brian. "This is not Mananaun's boat!"

"O Brother," said Enya, "the Ocean-Sweeper has as many shapes as the cloak of Mananaun has colours. Step into the boat."

When Brian had taken his place in the boat there was plenty of room, and when all the three were seated there was plenty of room, and the boat began to shine like a white crystal and the waves made a song of greeting as they lapped about the prow."

"Farewell!" said the sons of Turann; "keep gladness in your hearts till we come back."

The Ocean-Sweeper sprang from the shore like a sea-bird and wheeled and circled in the foam, waiting the word of command.

"Go to the Garden of the Golden Apple Tree that is guarded by dragons in the Eastern Half of the World," said Brian, and the Ocean-Sweeper sped swiftly forth.

The Garden of the Golden Apple Trees was very far off, and as they went to it the sons of Turann took counsel as to how they should get the apples.

"Let two of us," said Urcar, "make good sword's play on the dragons whilst the third gathers the apples."

"Yes," said Ur, "and when the apples are got, we three will slay the dragons and fight our way out of the garden."

"Wisdom is not in your words," said Brian, "we three would leave our bones among the dragons. Let us change ourselves into hawks and swoop on the apples from above."

"That is good," said the others. And when they were come to the garden they rose in the air, three golden hawks, and swooping on the tree took each an apple. The dragons were powerless to hinder them, but three of the maidens that walked in the garden – and each one was a king's daughter – changed themselves into fierce sharp-clawed griffins and followed the hawks. They could not overtake the hawks: and when they saw that, they held themselves motionless in the air and great flashes of light came from their angry eyes. They blew out three streams of fire after the hawks. The hawks plunged into the water and became three salmon, and when they reached the Ocean-Sweeper they leaped into it and took their own shapes.

"It is well we have the Apples of Healing," said Ur, "the witchfire has burnt us to the bone!"

They healed themselves with the apples and set out to seek the other treasures. It is long and long they were seeking them. They had foam of the Eastern World and foam of the Western World under their prow. They saw the Stars of the North and the Stars of the South and the Stars that are under the Sea. They were searching through the blackness of night and the redness of dawn and all the colours of the day. They knew the singing wave that lifts adventurers to the heights of the world and the silent wave that casts them down to the hollows. It is long they were seeking the treasures.

They got the Spear of Victory. They got the Magic Skin. They got the Hound. They got the Seven Swine. They got the Chariot. Their hearts were filled with pride and stubbornness.

Lugh, walking in Ireland by the sea, knew that the sons of Turann had the treasures, and he thought that they could too easily give the shouts on Midkena's hill and be free of the eric-fine. He made a spell of forgetfulness to bring them back and take from their minds the memory of Midkena's hill.

He stooped to lay the spell on the sea, and as he stooped a wave broke over his hands and a broken water-reed tangled itself in his fingers. He lifted up the reed and straightened it. He remembered the little well with the nine crystal bubbles, and the tenderness of the earth came into his heart.

"O little reed," he said, "I will give the sons of Turann a chance. I will make another spell and if, when it reaches them, they remember the wrong they did the Earth, they will remember also the shouts on Midkena's hill."

He made a spell that had memory and forgetfulness in it and laid it on the sea, and it became a wave and travelled unbroken till it reached the boat of Mananaun. It rocked the boat softly, and the three sons of

Turann remembered their father's house, but they had no sorrow for the wrong done to the earth, and forgetfulness of Midkena's hill came upon them.

"A good welcome would we have now if we were in our father's house," said Brian, "and good would it be in the morning to slip our hounds for the chase."

"And good would it be in the evening," said Urcar, "to hear the sound of harps in our father's house. Let us go back to Ireland."

"Go back to Ireland," said Brian to the Ocean-Sweeper, and it leaped through the sea-foam towards the Sacred Land.

On a height that looked far over the sea stood Turann's watcher, his eyes on the horizon. Day and night, since the setting forth of Turann's sons, a watcher had stood there, looking seaward. Swift runners waited for his joy-shout, and beacon-fires stood ready for the flame. It was early morning, and the watcher saw the pale mists whiten and the sea stir itself and wrinkle. Suddenly a great star rose in the horizon – it flashed; and grew; and neared. The watcher knew the Ocean-Sweeper. He leaped high for gladness of heart, and shouted:

"They come! They come! Turann's sons are returning!"

The cry was caught by the runners. They leaped and ran, and the joy-fires leaped and sparkled, blood-red in the paleness of morning. The joy-shout spread from mouth to mouth, and all that country rejoiced at the home-coming.

Turann went down to the edge of the sea to greet his sons, and Enya went with him and all the folk of the clan. Right glad were the three brothers to set their feet on Irish land. They showed the strange spoils, the marvellous eric fine they had brought for Lugh, and all that saw them wondered.

News of the home-coming was sent to Lugh by swift messengers, and he said: "Let the sons of Turann come and count the eric-fine before me."

The sons of Turann came before him, and with them came singing men and singing women and swordsmen and chariots and horsemen.

Brian counted out the eric-fine before Lugh.

Then Lugh said: "Good are the things ye have brought, but ye have not brought the full eric. Where is the cooking-spit that is a flame under the sea-wave?"

Then recollection came upon the sons of Turann, and they cried out:

"We are undone! We have not given the Shouts on Midkena's hill – we have not the Flame that is under the sea-wave!"

112

Shame burnt in the faces of all their kinsfolk because the sons of Turann had not the full eric, and they said: "Give the Ocean-Sweeper again, O Lugh, and the sons of Turann will pay the eric in full."

"Nay," said Lugh, "I lent the boat at first that the battle-loss of Cian might be made good in the great fight. The loss is made good." He bent his eyes on the sons of Turann, and said: "Ye are here now because my spell has brought you. I laid a spell of forgetfulness upon the sea, but the earth put with it a spell of remembrance, and if ye had remembered the wrong ye did the Earth, ye would have remembered the shouts on Midkena's hill, and easily would ye have given them since ye had the Spear of Victory, the Skin of Healing, and the Apples of Life. Now ye must fare forth without these treasures and without the boat of Mananaun, and whatsoever ye win ye will win solely by the strength that is in yourselves."

Then said Brian: "It is well named you are, Lugh the Long-Handed. Your vengeful fingers have reached across the sea to grasp us, and they will not loose their hold till you have dragged us under the grave-mound!"

Turann would have spoken, but Brian said to him: "Words are wasted, my Father; let us go." Sorrowfully they went homeward, and their thoughts were on the pathless sea.

Turann made ready a boat for his sons; thick-planked and strong, a boat with crimson sails. He proffered them rowers and men at arms, but they refused, because they were going they knew not whither, and were under a curse.

They stepped into the boat, they spread the crimson sails, and as they slid away from the land, all their people made lamentation for them.

"The Eagles are going!" they wailed. "The High Noble-hearted Ones, the Three Flames on the hearth of Turann. The lights are quenched to-night in the chieftain's house!"

The sons of Turann went searching for the Island of Caer, the Land that is under the Sea-Wave. They heard tidings of it in many places, but no one knew where it could be found. Wise Druids told them that the Island was protected by the magic of Fand, the Sea-Queen, the daughter of Flidias, and no one who went there ever returned.

The sun had risen and set many times on the search. Brian, Urcar and Ur were weary; the wind had failed them, and they were labouring at the oars: it seemed to them that they would never find the Island of Caer.

"Let us rest a little," said Urcar, "for my strength is spent."

They rested from the oars, and Brian cast a line over the side of the boat. He drew up a fish, white as silver and covered with crimson spots.

"Brother," said Ur, "your fish is purple-spotted like the Salmon that swims in Connla's Well and eats the crimson nuts of the Hazel of Knowledge: let him go free for sake of his beauty."

Brian threw the fish back to the water, and suddenly knowledge came to him, and he cried: "I know that the Island of Caer is beneath us!"

He jumped into the water and became a white stone, falling, falling, till he reached the Land that is Under the Sea. It was a goodly land and Brian took his own shape and walked through its starry meadows till he came to the Palace of the Guarded Flame. He entered it and found many beautiful maidens singing and broidering golden flowers on mantles for the daughter of Flidias. In the midst of them leaped and shone the Guarded Flame. Brian spoke no word when he entered and the maidens did not lift their eyes to look at him. He took the flame in his two hands and turned to leave the palace. The maidens burst out laughing.

"You are a brave man," they said, "and since the flame does not burn you, keep it. We have a flame for every day in the year, and you are the bravest champion and the handsomest that ever came to look at us broidering cloaks for the sea-queen."

"O Maidens," said Brian, "May every day in the year bring you fresh laughter and delight, and if good wishes can reach you from the country above the sea-floor ye will have mine every day I live, and farewell now, and my thousand blessings with you!"

He rose through the water till he came to where his brothers were and climbed into the boat. When the Flame came above the water it changed into a cooking-spit, and Brian laid it carefully in the boat.

"Our luck," he said, "is like sunshine in mid-winter, soon come, soon gone. Let us hasten to Midkena's Hill."

Midkena's Hill was very high and green. It rose almost straight out of the sea. Only on one side could it be climbed. On that side Midkena and his three sons were.

It was a great fight that the sons of Turann made with the Champions of the Hill. They were like fierce eagles contending together, and like bulls whose tramplings shake the earth. The demons of the air and the fierce creatures that live under the earth gathered to watch them fighting – and no one ever travelled over the nine ridges of the world to look at a fight that was better than that fight. Brian and his brothers got the victory over Midkena and his sons. They left them dead on the hill, but they themselves had barely strength to give the three shouts. When they had given the shouts weakness came on them, and they fell down and could not rise. Then Ur saw the demons of the air that have no pity and the fierce ones from under the earth watching him, and he said: "O my brothers, I would we were in our own country, lying on a hill-side there, for the Irish hills are gentle, and every wind that blows on them is full of peace."

"We have no part in Ireland," said Brian, "for we have broken the Great Oath."

"My grief!" said Urcar. "My bitter sorrow that we shall never see the Sacred Land again!"

While he spoke, a little wind came out of Ireland. It was very soft and gentle. It touched the sons of Turann, and there was so much healing in its touch that they rose up and stood on their feet.

"It is a wind surely from Ireland that has come to us," said Urcar, "let us make haste while we have strength and get to the boat."

They got down to the boat. They took the fastenings from it. They hoisted slowly the crimson sails, and the little wind strengthened itself and filled the sails and kept the boat before it till the hills of Ireland showed themselves like pale clouds.

"My blessing on the hills!" said Brian, and because he had the most strength he lifted up his brothers to get sight of the Irish land.

"It is good," they said, "to see Ben Eclair: our eyes were never more glad of it, and let us steer now to the haven where our father's house is."

Turann's watcher saw them afar off and raised the shout for them, and their kinsfolk and comrades waded into the sea and drew the boat to land. They lifted up the sons of Turann and would have carried them into their father's dun, but Brian said to them: "Lay us all three on the green grass, for we are hurt past any hope of healing, and send swift runners to Lugh that we may say to him before we die: 'The sons of Turann have paid you the full eric.'"

The three were laid on the green grass, and Enya, their sister, tended them, and the leeches and healers of their clan ministered unto them. Turann, their father, sat on the earth beside them: he was putting together, in his mind, words to say to Lugh.

When Lugh came, he was so fair and had such radiance about him that it seemed to every one he must have come newly out of Tir-nan-Oge.

Turann bowed himself before Lugh, and said: "O Mighty One, my sons have paid your eric in full, and never since the mountains lifted their heads above the waters has such an eric been asked for or paid. Grant now the Skin of Healing, that my sons may live."

Lugh came to where the sons of Turann were lying. He looked at them. There was neither pity nor anger in his face.

"My brothers," he said, "life is either a king's robe or a beggar's cloak. Do ye desire to live?"

The sons of Turann raised themselves and their hero-souls came back to them, so that they stood on their feet and cared not for their wounds.

"Ildana," they said, "We salute you! Win victory for us in the Great Battle even as you will win it for Cian. We do not covet the beggar's robe."

They turned and took farewell of their father, and their sister, and their kinsfolk. And they knelt and kissed the sacred earth, and said: "O Father, and O kinsfolk, entreat forgiveness for us from the earth, and friendly burial – even as we now entreat it for ourselves. Farewell. Make no lamentation for us."

But Turann and all his folk made a great lamentation.

In Tir-na-Moe, the Land of the Living Heart, Cian, son of Dian-Cecht, walked among the crimson lilies. His face was radiant and he had a branch with three golden apples in his hand. Faint sweet music was everywhere throughout that joyous country. Cian lifted up his eyes and saw the three sons of Turann approaching. They had the brightness of the morning about them and there was no wound on them. Cian went to meet them.

"Greeting," he said, "and welcome to Moy Mell."

He gave to each of them a golden apple. And when Brian, Ur, and Urcar had tasted of those apples they knew everything that had ever happened in the world and everything that would happen. They knew that the Fomor would be defeated in the Great Battle: they knew the words of the Peace-Chant that Brigit would sing:

"Peace up to Heaven,
Heaven down to earth.
The earth under Heaven.
Strength to every one."

"O Cian, dear Comrade," said the sons of Turann, "it is not hard to wait for news of victory in Moy Mell."

THE GOLDEN FLY

Ethaun, Angus, Fuamach, and Midyir lived in the World of the Gods. Ethaun said to Angus:

"I am weary of everything that I see; let me go into the other worlds with you."

Angus said:

"When I go into the other worlds I wander from place to place and people do not know that I am a god. In the earth they think I am a juggler or a wandering minstrel or a beggar-man. If you come with me you will seem a poor singing woman or a strolling player."

Then Ethaun said:

"I will ask Midyir to make a world for myself – all the worlds are full of weariness."

She went to find Midyir, and as she went she saw below her the World of the Bright Shadow that is called Ildathach, and the World of the Dark Shadow that is called Earth. Midyir was looking down at the Earth, and a brightness grew on it as he looked. Ethaun was angry because Midyir cared to make a brightness on the Earth, and she turned away from him, and said:

"I wish the worlds would clash together and disappear! I am weary of everything I can see."

Then Fuamach said:

"You have the heart of a fly, that is never contented; take the body of a fly, and wander till your heart is changed and you get back your own shape again."

Ethaun became a little golden fly, and she was afraid to leave the World of the Gods and wished she could get back her shape again. She flew to Midyir and buzzed round him, but he was making a brightness on the Earth and did not hear her; when she lit on his hand he brushed her away.

She went to Angus, and he was making music on the strings of his tiompan; when she buzzed about him he said: "You have a sweet song, little fly," and he made the tiompan buzz like a fly. She lit on his hand, and he said: "You are very beautiful, little golden fly, and because you are beautiful I will give you a gift. Now speak and ask for the gift that will please you best." Then Ethaun was able to speak, and she said:

"O Angus, give me back my shape again. I am Ethaun, and Fuamach has changed me into a fly and bidden me wander till I get back my shape."

Angus looked sadly at the little golden fly, and said: "It is only in Ildathach that I am a Shape-Changer. Come with me to that land and I will make a palace for you and while you are in it you will have the shape of Ethaun."

"I will go with you," said Ethaun, "and live in your palace."

She went with him, and he brought her into a beautiful palace that had all the colours of the rainbow. It had four windows to it, and when she looked out of the window to the West she saw a great wood of pine trees and oak trees and trees that had golden apples; when she looked out of the window to the North she saw a great mountain shaped like a spear, and white like flame; and when she looked to the South she saw a far-stretching plain with many little gleaming lakes; but the window to the East was fast closed, and Angus said she must never unbar it.

Ethaun was happy for a long time in the rainbow-palace and Angus came and played to her and told her tales of all the worlds; but at last the old longing came to her and she grew weary of everything she could see.

"I wish the walls of the palace would fall and the trees wither," she said, "for they are always the same!"

She went to the window in the East and unbarred it. She saw the sea outside it, wind-driven and white with foam, and a great wind blew the window open and caught Ethaun and whirled her out of the palace, and she became again a little golden fly. She wandered and wandered through the World of the Bright Shadow that is called Ildathach till she came to the World of the Dark Shadow that is Earth, and she wandered there for a long time, scorched by the sun and beaten by the rain, till she came to a beautiful house where a king and queen were standing together. The king had a golden cup full of mead and he was giving it to the queen. Ethaun lit on the edge of the cup, but the queen never saw the little golden fly, and she did not know that it slipped into the mead, and she drank it with the mead.

Afterwards there was a child born to the queen – a strange beautiful child, and the queen called her Ethaun. Every one in the palace loved the child and tried to please her but nothing pleased her for long and as she grew older and more beautiful they tried harder to please her but she was never contented. The queen was sad at heart because of this, and the sadness grew on her day by day and she began to think her child was of the Deathless Ones that bring with them too much joy or too much sorrow for mortals.

One day Ethaun said the queen's singer had no songs worth listening to and she began to sing one of her own songs; as she sang, the queen looked into her eyes and knew that Ethaun was no child of hers, and when she knew it she bowed herself in her seat and died. The king said Ethaun brought ill-luck and he sent her away to live in a little hut of woven branches in a forest where only shepherds and simple people came to her and brought her food.

She grew every day more beautiful and walked under the great trees in the forest and sang her own songs. One day the king of all Ireland came riding by. His name was Eochy, and he was young and beautiful and strong. When he saw Ethaun he said:

"No woman in the world is beautiful after this one!" And he got down from his horse and came to Ethaun. She was sitting outside the little hut and combing her hair in the sunshine, and her hair was like fine gold and very long.

"What is your name?" said the king, "and what man is your father?"

"Ethaun is my name," said she, "and a king is my father."

"It is wrong," said Eochy, "that your beauty should be shut in this forest, come with me and you shall be the High Queen of Ireland."

Then Ethaun looked at Eochy, and it seemed to her that she had known him always. She said: "I have waited here for you and no other. Take me into your house, High King."

Eochy took her with him and made her his queen, and all the country that he ruled was glad because the High Queen was so beautiful. Eochy made a wonderful house for her. It had nine doors of carved red yew, and precious stones were in the walls of it. Ethaun and the king lived in it, and the harpers sang to them, and the noblest warriors in Erin stood about their doors. The king was happy, but there was always in the mind of Ethaun a beauty that made the rich hangings seem poor and the jewels dull and she had a song in her heart that took the music out of all other songs. The harpers of the Five Provinces of Ireland came into the feast hall of Eochy at Samhain, but there was weariness on the face of Ethaun while they played, and though the High King gave them gold rings and jewels and high seats of honour they had no joy in coming to his house.

The warriors clashed their swords when the High Queen passed but any one who looked into her eyes dreamed of strange countries and had in him the longing to go over seas, and Eochy was grieved because the noblest of his chiefs became like the lonely bird of the waves that never builds a nest.

One day Ethaun leaned against the carved yew door of her sunny-palace and watched the seagulls wheeling in the blueness of the sky. Inside, the Fool was strewing green rushes and scented leaves and buds before her chair. The Fool was always in the palace because his wits had gone from him, and people say that fools have the dark wisdom of the gods. Ethaun could hear him singing:

"I had a black hound and a white.
The Day is long, and long the Night.

A great wave swallowed up the sea,
And still the hounds were following me.

The white hound had a crown of gold,
But no one saw it, young or old.

The black hound's feet were swift as fire —
'Tis he that was my heart's desire.

The Sun and Moon leaned from the sky
When I and my two hounds went by."

Ethaun turned from the door and went into the room where the Fool was. Her dress swept the young green leaves but she had no thought of them or of the little flowers the Fool had put with the rushes.

"Go on singing!" she said. "I wish my heart were as lightsome as yours."

"How could your heart be lightsome, Queen," said the Fool, "when you will not give the flower a chance to blossom, or the hound a chance to catch his prey, or the bird a clear sky to sing in? If you were of the Deathless Ones you would burn the world to warm your hands!"

The redness of shame spread itself in Ethaun's face. She stooped and lifted a little bud from the floor.

"I think the Deathless Ones could make this bud blossom," she said, "but all the buds that I break off wither in my hands. I will break no more buds, Fool."

While she spoke there was a noise outside, and Ethaun asked her women what it was.

"Only a beggar-man they are driving away. He says he is a juggler and can do tricks."

"Let him stay," said Ethaun, "and I will see his tricks."

"O Queen," said the women, "he is a starveling and ignorant; how could he please you when Incar, the King's juggler, did not please you?"

120

"Let the man stay," said Ethaun; "if he has the will to please me he will please – and to-night Incar will please me too."

She stepped out through the carved yew door and bade the beggar-man do his tricks. He was clumsy and his tricks were not worth looking at, but the Queen gave him a ring from her finger and the little bud she had in her hand, and said: "Stay here to-night and the King's juggler will teach you good feats."

The beggar-man put the ring in his bosom but he kept the bud in his hands and suddenly it blossomed into a rose and he plucked the petals apart and flung them into the air and they became beautiful white birds and they sang till every one forgot the sky above them and the earth beneath them with gladness, but Ethaun put her hands before her eyes and the tears came through her fingers.

The birds circled away into the air, singing, and when the people looked for the beggar-man he was gone. Ethaun called after him: "Angus! Angus! Come back!" But no one answered, and there was only the far-off singing of the birds.

That night the King's juggler did feats with golden balls and with whirling swords and Ethaun praised him so that for gladness he thought of new feats, and while the people were shouting with delight a tall dark man in the robes of a foreigner came into the hall. Now the king loved to speak with men from far countries and he called the stranger to him, and said: "What knowledge have you, and what skill is in your fingers?"

"I know," said the stranger, "where the sun goes when the earth does not see it, and I have skill in the playing of chess."

Gladness was on the king when he heard of the chess playing, for he himself had such skill that no one could beat him.

"I will play a game with you," he said. "Let the chess-board be brought."

"O King," said the attendants, "there is only the Queen's chess-board, and it is locked away because she said it was not beautiful."

"I will go myself for the board," said the king, and he rose up to get it.

The stranger brought out a chessboard that had the squares made of precious stones brighter than any stones of the earth and he set the men on it. They were of gold and ivory, but the ivory was whiter than the whiteness of a cloud and the gold brighter than the sunset.

"I will give you this board in exchange for yours," he said to the queen.

"No," said Ethaun, "the board that Eochy made for me I will keep."

"I will make something for you, too," said the stranger. "I will make worlds for you." Ethaun looked into his eyes, and she remembered the

World of the Gods, and Midyir, and Angus, and Fuamach, and how she had been a little golden fly.

"O Midyir," she said, "in all the worlds I would be nothing but a little fly. I have wandered far, but I have learned wisdom at last from a Fool. I am going to make a world for myself."

As she was speaking Eochy came back with the board.

"The first games on my board," said Midyir, "the last on yours."

"Be it so," said Eochy. Midyir began to set out the men. "What are we playing for?" said Eochy.

"Let the winner decide," said Midyir.

Eochy won the first game, and he asked for fifty horses out of fairyland.

"I will get them," said Midyir, and they played again. Eochy won, and he said: "I will ask for four hard things. Make a road over Moin Lamraide; clear Mide of stones; cover the district of Tethra with rushes; and the district of Darbrech with trees."

"When you rise in the morning stand on the little hill near your house and you will see all these things done," said Midyir. They played again, and Midyir won.

"What do you ask?" said Eochy.

"I ask Ethaun," said Midyir.

"I will never give her!" said Eochy.

"The horses of fairyland are trampling outside your door, O King," said Midyir, "give me my asking." And he said to Ethaun:

"Will you come into your own world again?"

Ethaun said: "There is no world of all the worlds my own, for I have never made a place for myself, but Eochy has made a place for me and all the people have brought me gifts, and for the space of a year I will stay with them and bring them gladness."

"I will come at the year's end," said Midyir, and he left the hall, but no man saw him go.

After that there was never such a year in Ireland. The three crowns were on the land – a crown of plenty, a crown of victory, and a crown of song. Ethaun gave gifts to all the High King's people, and to Eochy she gave a gladness beyond the dream of a man's heart when it is fullest; and at Samhain time Eochy made a great feast and the kings of Ireland and the poets and the druids were there, and gladness was in the heart of every one.

Suddenly there was a light in the hall that made the torches and the great candles that are lit only for kings' feasts burn dim, and Midyir the Red-Maned stood in the hall. Then the ollavs and the poets and the druids and chiefs bowed themselves, and the king bowed himself, because Midyir had come. Midyir turned his eyes to where Ethaun sat in a seat of carved silver by the king. He had a small cruit such as musicians carry and he made a sweet music on it and sang:

Come with me! Come with me! Ethaun,
Leave the weary portals of life, leave the doon,
 leave the bawn.
  Come ! Come ! Come ! Ethaun.
Lo! the white-maned untameable horses, out-racing
 the wind,
Scatter the embers of day as they pass, and the
 riders who bind
The suns to their chariot wheels and exult are
 calling your name,
Are calling your name through the night, Ethaun,
 and the night is a-flame,
  Ethaun ! Ethaun ! Ethaun !
Come with us, Ethaun, to Moy-Mell where the
 star-flocks are straying
Like troops of immortal birds for ever delaying,
 delaying
The moment of flight that would take them away
 from the honey-sweet plain.
Surely you long for waves that break into starry rain
And are fain of flowers that need not die to blossom again.
Why have you turned away from me your only lover?
What lure have you seen in the eyes of a mortal
 that clay must cover?
Come back to me! Come back, Ethaun! The high-built heavenly
 places
Mourn for you, and the lights are quenched, and
 for you immortal faces
Grow wan as faces that die. 0 Flame-Fair Swan of Delight,
Come with me, leave the weary portals of sleep-
 heavy Night;
The hosts are waiting, their horses trample the
 ashes of day;
Come, Light of a World that is Deathless, come away!
 Come away!

Midyir stretched his hands to Ethaun, and she turned to Eochy and kissed him.

"I have put into a year the gladness of a long life," she said, "and to-night you have heard the music of Faery, and echoes of it will be in the harp-strings of the men of Ireland for ever, and you will be remembered as long as wind blows and water runs, because Ethaun – whom Midyir loved – loved you."

She put her hand in Midyir's and they rose together as flame rises or as the white light rises in the sky when it is morning; and in the World of the Gods Angus waited for them, and Fuamach; and they walked together again as they had walked from the beginning of time.

THE LUCK CHILD

Aidan, Osric, and Teigue, were the cow-herds of Eterscel, the High King of Ireland. Aidan was old and gentle, Osric was young and fierce, Teigue was an *omadhaun* – a fool – they watched the cattle of the king and chased the wild beasts from them. At night they slept in little wicker huts on the edge of the forest.

One day as Teigue was gathering dry sticks for his fire he saw a very young child lying wrapped in a mantle at the foot of a pine tree. He went over to the child and it smiled in his face. He left off gathering sticks and sat down beside it. Osric came to see what was keeping Teigue.

"A fool's errand is long a-doing," he said. "What are you loitering here for, when the meat is waiting for the fire and the fire is waiting for the sticks?"

"I have here," said Teigue, "what is better than meat, a gift from the Hidden People." Osric looked at the child.

"We have little use for a nine-months' infant," he said.

The child smiled at him.

"Where could we keep it?" he asked Teigue.

"I will make a house for it," said Teigue, "a little house in the middle of the forest, that no one can find but myself."

"'Tis a pity the child should perish in the forest," said Osric. "Of a truth the house must be built."

Aidan came. He lifted the child in his arms and looked at the mantle wrapped about it. The mantle was thickly embroidered with gold flowers.

"This is the child of some queen," he said. "One day great folk will come seeking her."

"I will not let the great folk take her away," said Teigue. "She is my Luck-Child. She is Osric's Luck-Child too, and we are going to make a house for her, and she will bring us good luck every day of our lives."

"She is my Luck-Child too," said Aidan. "We three will make a secret house in the forest, and there we will keep her from prying eyes."

They sought out a place, a hidden green spot in the forest. They made a house, and there they nurtured the child in secret. Year by year she throve and grew with them. Teigue brought her berries and taught her to play on a little reed flute. When she made music on it the wild creatures of the woods came about her. She played with the spotted fawns, and the king of the wolves crouched before her and licked her hands. Osric made a bow for her, and taught her how to shoot with arrows, but she had no wish to kill any beast, for all the forest-creatures were her friends. Aidan told her stories. He told her how the sun changed into a White Hound at night, and Lugh the Long-Handed put a silver chain on it and led it away to his Secret Palace, and it crouched at his feet till the morning, when he loosed it and let it run through the sky again. He told her how Brigit counted the stars so that no littlest one got lost, and how she hurried them away in the morning before Lugh's great hound came out to frighten them. He said that Brigit came in the very early mornings to gather herbs of healing, for it was she who gave the secret of healing to wise physicians, and it was she gave power and virtue to every herb that grows. He said that once the High King's Poet had seen Brigit and had made a song about her and called her 'The Pure Perpetual Ashless Fire of the Gael.'

The Luck-Child loved to hear Aidan's stories. She loved them even when she had grown quite tall and wise and was no longer a child.

Teigue was sorry that she grew up so quickly. He sat down one day and began to lament and cry Ochone! about it.

"Why are you lamenting and crying Ochone?" said Osric.

"Because my Luck-Child has grown up and the Hidden People will see that she is no longer a child. They will take her and make her a queen amongst them, and she will never come back to us. Ochone, Ochone!"

"If the chiefs and warriors of King Eterscel do not see her," said Osric, "she is safe enough: and if they do come to take her I will not let her go without a fight."

Aidan heard them talking.

"Do not speak of trouble or sorrow when you speak of the Luck-

Child," he said. "One day she will come to her own. And then she will give each of us his heart's wish."

"I will wish for a robe all embroidered with gold," said Teigue. "What will you wish for, Osric?"

"For a shield and spear and the right to go into battle with warriors."

"What will you wish for, Aidan?

"I will wish, O Teigue, to sit in the one dun with the Luck-Child, and hear the poets praising her."

"I will go and tell the Luck-Child our wishes," said Teigue, "so that she may know when she comes to her own."

He ran to the little hut in the forest, and the Luck-Child came out to meet him. She laughed to hear of the wishes, and said she would have a wish herself in the day of good fortune, and it would be to have Teigue, Osric, and Aidan, always with her. She took a little reed flute and began to play on it.

"Listen now," she said to Teigue, "and I will play you music I heard last night when the wind swept down from the hills."

Teigue sat under a pine tree and listened.

A great white hound came through the wood, and when it saw Teigue it stood and bayed. The hound had **a** gold collar set with three crystal stones.

"O my Luck-Child," said Teigue, "a king will come after this hound. Go quickly where he can get no sight of you."

She had the will to go, but the hound bayed about her feet and would not let her move. A clear voice called the hound, and through the trees came the High King of Ireland: there was no one with him but his foster-brother.

The king had the swiftness and slenderness of youth on him. 'Tis he that was called the Candle of Beauty in Tara of the Kings – and nowhere on the yellow-crested ridge of the world could his equal be found for hardiness and high-heartedness and honey-sweet wisdom of speech.

His foster-brother had a thick twist of red gold in his hair, and he was the son of a proud northern king. The Luck-Child seemed to both of them a great wonder.

"What maiden is this?" said the king, and stood looking at her.

"She is my Luck-Child, O King," said Teigue.

"She is no child of thine!" said the king's foster-brother.

"She is a child of the Hidden People," said Teigue, "and she has brought me luck every day since I found her."

"Tell me," said the king, "how you found her."

"I found her under a pine tree, a nine-months' child wrapped in a mantle all sewn over with little golden flowers. She is my Luck-Bringer since that day."

"She is mine to-day!" said the king. "O Luck-Child," he said, "will you come and live in my palace and bring me good fortune? It is you will be the High Queen of Ireland, and you will never have to ask a thing the second time."

"Will you give Teigue a gold-embroidered robe and let him stay always with me?"

"I will do that," said the king.

"Will you give Osric a sword and let him go into battle like a warrior?"

"Who is Osric?

"It was Osric who built the house for me and taught me to shoot with arrows and speared salmon in the rivers for me. I will not go with you without Osric."

"I will give Osric what you ask," said the king, "let him come to me."

"I will bring him," said Teigue, and he ran to find Osric and Aidan.

"O Foster-Brother," said the king, "it is well we lost our way in the woods, for now I have found the queen the druids promised me. 'Good luck,' said they, 'will come to King Eterscel when he weds a queen of unknown lineage.' It is this maiden who will bring me luck."

He took the Luck-Child by the hand, and they went through the wood with the hound following them.

Soon they met Teigue, Osric, and Aidan, coming together. The Luck-Child ran to them and brought them to the king.

"Here is Osric," she said, "and Aidan who told me stories."

"I will give Osric one of my own war-chariots and his choice of weapons," said the king. "What am I to give to Aidan?

"Is there a carved seat in your palace where he can sit and listen to your poet who made the song about Brigit?"

"There are many carved seats in my palace, and he shall sit in one," said Eterscel. "All the three shall sit in seats of honour, for they will be the Foster-Fathers of the High Queen of Ireland."

He turned to the three cow-herds.

"On the day ye built the little hut in the forest for your nursling ye built truth into the word of my druids, and now I will build honour into your fortune. Ye shall rank with chiefs and the sons of chiefs. Ye shall drink mead in feast-halls of your own, and while I live ye shall have my goodwill and protection."

"May honour and glory be with you forever, O King," said Aidan. "In a good hour you have come to us."

"We are all going to the palace," said the Luck-Child. "Teigue, where is your flute?"

"It is in the little hut," said Teigue. "I will go back for it."

"Nay," said the king, "there are flutes enough in the palace! I will give you one of silver, set with jewels."

The Luck-Child clapped her hands for joy.

"I love you," she said to the king. "Come, let us go!"

She took Teigue by the one hand and the king by the other, and they all went to the palace. Every one wondered at the Luck-Child, for since the days of Queen Ethaun, who came out of Fairyland, no one so beautiful was seen in Ireland. The king called her Ethaun, and all the people said that in choosing her he had done well.

There was feasting and gladness on the day they swore troth to each other, and Teigue said the sun got up an hour earlier in the morning and stayed an hour later in the sky that night for gladness.

SMOKE OF MYRRH
(1950)

The poems included here were written late in Ella's life. In poetic form she brings us magical incantations drawn from ancient Irish myth, a sparse and powerful farewell to her native land, and richly evoked images of the world of Faery. She reminds us that what is truly and deeply felt remains with us forever – surely Ella was a Walker Between the Worlds.

THE SALMON OF KNOWLEDGE

Give us luck, Grey Standing Stone.
For we are fisher-folk.

Now, osier-stirred,
Thrice, and twice, is Sionaun's Well.

Give us luck, Dark Well.

Down,
Down,
Far down:
Like a star
Like a moon
Like a gold-plumed bird
In these shadowed deeps
Fintan the Salmon sleeps.

Hoy - - ee – sha!

He will rise at a word,
Glittering up through the waters,
Lighting the dark waters.

Rise, Hoy - - ee – sha!
Rise, Hoy - - ee – sha!

Waken from your sleep
Jewel of the Deep
Rise with slow-winnowing fins!

Rise! Rise! Rise!
If we could snare him
We'd have the world for prize!
Or, better, we'd not care
For any kingdom there:
Both grown so wise.

CLOUDED SKY

What a stir the wind is making!
Riving, breaking,
The boughs of the forest.
The sea is tossed
Up-caught and lost
In wind-torn spume.

A day to sit close in a room
By the ingle-neuk
And read from an old-world book
Of jousts and tourneys
Of perilous lone journeys
And the Sanctgreal quest;
To mouth such names as Agravaine,
Sire Palimonde, and Sire Gawaine,
With Sagramore and Tristagel;
Take note of Vivian who knew
Spells to make a wish come true;
Morgante, the queen, long unforgot;
Elaine, the maid of Astolat,
And demoiselles as fair:
Yolande, Etarre, and queen Iseulte,

With Camelot's queen Guinevere,
Their jewelled sleeves, their hoods of vair,
Their heavy lustrous braided hair,
Their castles set in flowering meads
By still grave waters, their white steeds,
Their stolen hounds of Faerylande.

Until dusk comes read happily
Of dragons and outlandish beasts,
Of wizards and bewitchment feasts
And haught adventures that maybe
No mortal had by land or sea:
Read, while the wind from the hill,
Riotous, tilts at the window-sill,
And the wave on the strand
Drags back in a flurry of sand.

GUERDON

Since you're away to the Spanish main
And your heart is on the deep,
What will you bring when you come again,
What gift for Love to keep?

A falcon white on your wrist to sit,
Sweet spices from Cathay,
A rope of pearls with rubies knit,
And a kyrtle green as May.

Make choice, make choice, of my gift to you
Ere your ship leans out to see:
Your good-luck wish upon my sword,
No better gift could be!

You might have asked for my lips on yours,
To hold me lief and fast.
Choose rather a wish on the sword, dear Love,
Untarnished, keen-edged, to the last!

131

ACHIEVEMENT

I have found the Well between the Seven Hazels
And drunk thereof.

I have climbed the Tower where the two Cranes
Keep watch
Beneath and above.

I have travelled with the wind, with wind-blown
Leaves, with water,
And wave-torn light.

I have snared the Salmon in the Pool of Knowledge,
And the Swan in flight.

GRAIL-QUEST

Since we can never win, what use the flight
Unless death-impact and death-pang make whole,
For one last feverish draught, the broken bowl?
To eyes long penned in murk a taper's light
May seem the sun – or yet more glorious sight:
We who would have for eucharist the soul
Touch it with starving lips, a moment's dole.
From depth of sorrow gage ecstatic height!

Ah, well we know the low safe-trodden path
Would shield us from the storm, and yet we choose
The high adventure and the torn sea's wrath!
Paying in agony the venture's dues.
So is the Tree of Life struck deep in Hell
That Paradisal fruits may bud and swell.

Ella Young, in her Garden, Oceano, California, no date.
Photograph by Ansel Adams.

EIRE

It is farewell now, a long and lasting farewell,
To the Land that nurtured me,
Mother and goddess.

A wood that I loved will remember:
A mountain that looks sea-ward will not forget me.

I shall not forget the last greenness,
Nor two sea-hawks circling, circling,
In the pale morning sky.

FOLK OF DANA

Lords of the Air,
The beautiful sons of the goddess,
Are driving the tempest tonight:
Pitiless stinging rain
And blinding light.

Ah, the wild glad laughter,
The wild proud throng!

They lean on the wind,
They cry to each other
Exulting in power,
Brother with brother
Beautiful and ruthless.

My eyes had sight of them
In a bye-gone hour:
Looked once, looked long,
And turned away.
I will go out now
Where the great trees thunder and sway,
Bough groaning to bough.

They may pass over,
I may see the wonder,
The hurrying splendour again,
The sons of the goddess
Beautiful and ruthless,
Brightness that age cannot dim
Nor the grave-mould stain.

See the Branch, the Branch a-flower,
And what steeds they hold,
Whiter than leaping fire,
Brighter than gold!

SONG OF A FAERY LOVER

Swan from the air
Leaf from the bough,
With the Bell-Branch I carry
I charm to me now:
Silver-throated swinging
The bells of it are ringing
Like faery birdlets singing
All so happily.

Hear the faint sweet chiming,
Cadenced and climbing,
Close wound, yet free,
And for sound of the Bell-Branch
Follow me!
Oh follow
O'er foam-crest and hollow.

My white steeds are biding,
Their long manes sliding,
In a wave-curl of the sea.

Hark to their neighing!

The shaken wave,
The shore wave swaying,
Sinks to the sea:
The wave returns,
Return with me.

I charm your eyes,
I charm your feet,
I charm your heart
With mine to beat,
Flame to white flame
Austere and fair.

I charm you to diviner air.

I am laughter of the sea,
I bear the Bell-Branch,
Follow me!

ARTEMIS

The moon took off her mask for me
Yester-night,
I saw her strange face
Ivory-white.

Crouching in the jungle, too,
The leopard saw:
And stretched in haughty greeting
A scimitar claw.

THE TANGLE-COATED HORSE
(1929)

In this collection, Ella Young turned to one of the best loved story cycles of Ireland – the adventures of Fionn Mac Cumhail, warrior and poet and leader of an extraordinary band of heroes: the Fianna. As with all her writings Ella Young brought her own special touches to these tales – but she also respected the traditional stories, which can still be read today in collections like the Fianagecht *where the origins of most of this set of stories can be found. The richness and beauty of the language, its vivid tones and poetic arches seem to us as fine an example of writing as one could find anywhere.*

A NIGHT OF THE NIGHTS

A small boy sat under an oak tree in a forest of oaks. Sunburnt of face and body he was for his deerskin tunic covered little of him. His blue eyes had a steady look in them like the eyes of a hawk and his thick mane of hair was a bright red-gold. He was pounding a deerskin with a smooth rounded stone to soften it: mayhap for sake of a tunic, or a pair of thonged shoes. He was alert as a forest creature – that child – for the snapping of a twig brought him to his feet, listening like a fawn. A tall woman with a deeply lined face and black hair that had many a strand of grey in it was coming through the trees:

"Fionn," she said, "my Treasure, is the skin a strong one?"

"It is, Bovemall," said the boy, "I have pounded it as you taught me: and softened it as well with my fingers."

"Good at skin-craft you are," said the woman, "you will know more things than your father knew, when you come to be chieftain of Clann Bassna."

"He had hounds to take the deer for him, and house-thralls to soften the skins," said the boy. "He would know how to ride a proud horse.

He had craft of a swordsman. Mayhap I will come by that and have my wood-craft to throw in with it."

"Mayhap you will," said the woman going to a little near-by clearing where the ashes of a fire were. She set to kindling a flame; and another woman – Liath her comrade – old like herself, came to help her.

Fionn continued to soften his deerskin, and his thoughts ran on the knowledge he had. He was a creature of the forest. He counted time by the blossoming and withering of the moon and by the burgeoning of leaves and their fluttering fall, pencilled and painted for their last dance with the wind. He knew how to track the forest creatures; and how to stand still suddenly, like a tree or a stone, the way they did. He knew how to make friends with them too. Bovemall had taught him that. And as he pounded his deerskin his thoughts went back to the day when she had shown him how to make friends with the wolves. She sat in a green place far in the heart of the forest. The trees stood in a circle about that green place and the wind went from tree-top to tree-top but did not come down to play in the grass. Open sky was above it. Bovemall made Fionn sit beside her. Then she began a low crooning song, a song without words in it. She clapped her hands together as she sang and swayed with the rhythm of her singing. Fionn was hard set to keep awake, till the sudden cry of a wolf startled sleep from him – a second wolf answered; then another, and another, till the forest was alive with voices. Then came pattering feet, and in the circle of the tree Fionn could see flashing eyes and the glint of white fangs and grey bodies slipping between the tree-trunks. Fionn did not dare to speak. Bovemall went on singing, and in the shadow of the forest those grey bodies slipped from tree-trunk to tree-trunk. *They* were silent but their feet made a padding rhythmic sound. Suddenly Bovemall stopped singing. She stood erect:

"Let the king of the wolves come hither," she said.

A great grey beast loped into the open space. He looked at Fionn, and the circle of trees, and his followers slipping from shadow to shadow, and at Bovemall – all in one glance – without seeming to look at anything.

"King of the wolves," said Bovemall, "this child is the chief of Clann Bassna. To day he is little and weak, but some day he will be strong and a great hunter able to smite your people or let them slip by unharmed. The forest protects him. He has earth-luck, and luck out of faeryland. To-day he would give friendship to you in exchange for your friendship."

Three times in token of friendship the great grey beast had circled Fionn, and three times in token of good-fellowship Fionn had circled the wolf: going carefully from left to right. Then Bovemall had poured between them a gift of wine and honey and milk, and called on the earth to witness – and on running water and sun and moon and wind – and so the pact was established. Fionn had kept that friendship. So had the wolves.

Bovemall had shown him many things. She had shown him how to coax the wind from its path in the tree-tops down to their fire of logs where it made patterns in the white wood ash: or lifted the Autumn leaves in a scarlet and golden swirl. Bovemall herself could call the wind out of a clear sky and send it crashing and hurtling through the forest. She could tame it at its fiercest, lulling it to sleep with softly spoken words. She could send it to shepherd the rain clouds, herding them to thirsty places: or withholding them. It was Bovemall who taught Fionn how to greet the water; running water that danced in streams and rivers; lake-water that moved silently among reeds and stony places, or lay darkly in the mountain-hollows. Fionn had seen the spirit of the water glitter like a dragon myriad-scaled and moving joyously; he had seen it laugh and blow a thousand colours from its lips, and he had laughed in answer calling out childish endearments to it; names that no one knew but himself.

Fionn thought of these things, and things kin to them, while he pounded his deerskin. He pounded it till the light slipped away and darkness like a quiet-footed army took the forest. Then Fionn folded his deerskin and laid it at the foot of the oak tree. He went to the fire in the clearing.

"Bovemall," he said, "is it likely that Moorna my mother will come hither on a day of these days?"

"There is no likelihood of her coming at all," said Bovemall. "Is it not enough that you saw her when the first buds reddened the forest, she that had to slip like a fox through watching hounds to visit you: is it likely that the king she wedded will give her leave a second time to risk the marshes and stony places – and pitfalls in the murk of moonless nights?"

"She came to me in a dream last night, Bovemall. Her face was very white: it may be that she is dead."

"That is a fool's thought. Moorna cannot die. She is of the Faery Folk and will go back to them when the time comes without a wrinkle in her fairness or a grey hair in the pride of her gold."

"She had tears in her eyes in my dream," said Fionn.

"Belike she had," cried Liath. "It's little she thought when she left the Plain of Honey to wed with Uail your father that had the look of a god on him, how soon she would be keening lost battles and her dead man!"

"Well," said Bovemall, "if the light in Aloon is quenched the candles are lit elsewhere for her. The king she has now spreads his share of the world under her feet."

"Are all the lights quenched indeed in Aloon?" asked Fionn. "You said it was the palace of a thousand candles."

"How can I tell?" said Bovemall. "It's Goll that has it now and its thousand candles if he cares to set flame to them; Goll that slew your father before you ever saw the light of day; Goll that wasted the Clann Bassna and left us without a roof to shelter us other than the branchy forest, and we going from lair to lair in it hunted and baited like badgers."

"When I am man-grown," said Fionn, "I will win back what my father had: it will be a hard day for Goll that day. I will kindle fire in Aloon and set the harpers playing."

"The Lordship of the Fianna of Ireland: that is what Uail had, and the friendship of the High King. It is not a vaunt or two that will win it, Fionn my Treasure."

"Don't be putting a hare's heart in the boy with ill-omened speech," said Liath. "It may be that the Salmon of Knowledge that winnows greenness to the earth, and life to every living creature, will winnow luck to Fionn."

"Liath," said Fionn, "I had Bovemall's word that she would tell me of that Salmon when the deerskin was softened. It is softened to-night: Bovemall, will you tell me of the Salmon?"

"I will indeed, my Golden Hawk: but first I must put the deer-meat under power of the embers."

She swept the burning flakes of wood from a hollow place by the fire; a hollow place lined with flat stones that were almost red-hot. She wrapped a piece of venison in a barth of sharptasting herbs, and placed it on the hot stones. Then she drew flaming embers over the hollow place.

"Soon you will have something to put your teeth in, Fionn," said Bovemall, "and now sit with your back to the big oak tree, for this is a long story, and I will tell you of the Pool of Wisdom that some call the Well of Knowledge; and of the Salmon that swims there."

Fionn sat with his back to the oak tree: and with the murmur of its leaves and the sound of the forest about them Bovemall told him of the Well of Knowledge:

"In the Heaven-World there is a Fountain that leaps up like a great feathered plume, like a tower of crystal, and falls back into itself and spreads and widens – deep; and deep; and deep – into a pool of delight. By the side of it the Sacred Hazel Trees are growing. They lift themselves so loftily and put forth their branches so lustily beyond eyesight that

140

no soul knows where an end comes to them: if end at all. Always in one joyous burgeoning they have leaves and fruit and blossom. Heavy-fruited clusters of nuts they have, scarlet and vermilion, and one by one they drop into the Pool when they have come to ripeness; stirring the waters, troubling them, till from their depths the Salmon rises. He is the Lord of the Pool. He is the Jewel of the Waters: every precious stone is his covering. Winnowing with mighty fins he rises, lighting the depths of the Pool with his brightness, scattering stars and star-fire in the eddies of his rising. One by one he swallows the nuts in their falling: they are the Hazels of Wisdom. They are the clustered Nuts of Knowledge: and the Salmon, that has gold of the sun and silver of the moon in every shining scale of him, is the Salmon of Knowledge:

Because of his joy in the Nuts, the Fountain leaps and renews itself:
It leaps and renews itself.
Because of the Fountain, the Hazels are blossoming
Dropping their fruits of scarlet in the Pool of Delight:
And winnowing there in the rain of their falling, vermilion-rinded and
golden, the Salmon is glad.
The Salmon is glad.
And glad for his sake is the Pool that forever leaps and renews itself.

"So there is never age on the Fountain; or weariness on the Salmon; or withering on the Sacred Hazels."

"Could I find that Pool, Bovemall; could I look into it?"

"That is not for me to say, Dear Heart. Great seers have seen it in their visions: but only the Shining Ones have power to walk by it, and look into it."

"Did any of the Shining Ones walk by it; did they look into it?"

"Yes, the Shining Ones walked there in the youth of the world; and before the world was fashioned at all: or even thought of. One or other of them would stand by the Hazel Trees and look into the Pool. They would see the Salmon that is the jewel of the waters; they would see their own unwithering beauty mirrored there and go thence contented. On a time Sive, most lovely of the Shining Ones, came to the Pool. She saw the Salmon winnowing there. She saw the image of her own beauty, but she was not satisfied. She struck the water with her hands and cried:

'Show me what secrets you keep in the black stillness where the Salmon has never dived: I would see the roots of the Sacred Hazels.'

"Then the pool was troubled and the waters burst forth and swept Sive down and down, deeper than the roots of the Sacred Hazels, deeper than the Abyss itself, until she came to the Earth – that was not Earth then – that had no shape or promise of trees nor any laughter of streams. Sive that is called Cassir took the Earth into her keeping; she made curves and whorls of beauty in the veins of its rocks, and patterns of beauty on its waters. She nourished and protected it till such a time as another of the Shining Ones came to the Pool. He looked into the depths, trusting to see some new thing; some portent of Sive it may be. He saw the Salmon, and the image of his own beauty.

'I would see the Abyss,' he cried, and he struck the waters: as Sive had struck them. They rose in a great surge and swept him down; and down. Powers and thrones and principalities descended with him in a splendid swirl. He was Partholan. He made trees grow upon the Earth, and set broad-leaved water-plants in the lakes that Sive had made. After him came Nemed, flamed and clouded with constellations. It was Nemed that had knowledge of the Crystal Tower that rears its head above the oceans of the world to the wheel of the stars. He knew the secret name of the sun and the titles of the moon. Then came the Folk of Dahna with the Four Jewels: the Sword of Light, the Cauldron of Plenty, the Spear of Victory, and the Stone of Destiny; the Talismans of four great Heaven-Cities. They never took the Jewels back to those four cities, nor did they themselves return. Their feet still gladden the Earth. The honey-bees know them. The swallows cry to them when they are making ready to follow Summer across the dark shoreless waters.

"And still the Shining Ones walked by the Pool, and cared for naught but their own beauty; till Miled came. We are of the race of Miled. The Folk that came with him build the cities of men and give knowledge to their druids and craft of hand to their smiths. Miled and all the Shining Ones have honour among men, for that they made trees and reed-fringed lakes and richness of corn and honey and fruits and pleasant beasts and birds upon the Earth: but Sive, that is named Cassir and who is also called Dahna, is the Mighty Mother. In honour of her the stars are lit. She tosses the sun in the palm of her hand. The moon is a plaything for her."

"She is too mighty to look upon," said Fionn, "she did not seem to be so big when she was Sive."

"She has still the name of Sive," said Bovemall, "and she is also called Brigit. She has more names than you could say over in all the hours of one day; and more shapes."

"Has she any shapes that are small shapes?"

"She has the shape of everything that lives. The shape of the berry on the tree; the shape of the wind that goes invisible. She is more invisible than the wind, for no one can track her by her foot-prints as one can track the wind."

"Has she still the shape of the Shining One that was Sive?"

"She has still that shape."

"Then one day I will travel and travel and travel till I come to the Pool, and maybe I will set eyes on Sive."

"It may be that you will set eyes on her," said Bovemall, "for who knows what the days and years of a lifetime will bring to anyone?"

Fionn sat very quiet for a while. He settled himself more comfortably against the tree. He shut his eyes tight, and saw a pool darker and bigger than the night-sky. The Salmon moved in it with every scale of him brighter than the sun, larger than the moon of harvest, full-orbed. He winnowed there with fins redder than larch-buds, scarlet, ruby-coloured like berries of the yew. Winnowing greenness to the Earth he was, and tempests and hail and flakes of snow and gentle rains and sunny days of Spring and Summer: and luck to Fionn.

And so Fionn slept with tight-shut eyes, till Bovemall waked him later when the venison was drawn from the embers.

THE MOON-BOWL

Messengers threaded their way at times through the forest to Bovemall; weather-beaten men who came secretly. Often after their coming Bovemall and Liath and Fionn moved to a new place in the forest, or found a deep cavern to lurk in for a while. Often Fionn would be told to greet the men. They would look eagerly upon him. They would salute him as the son of a chief should be saluted. They would call him the Young Hawk of Battle, and the Bull of Combats. They kissed the fringes of his ragged deerskin mantle; and one swart-faced man with gold rings in his ears pressed a smooth white queer-shaped bone into Fionn's hand, and said:

"This is a sea-beast's tooth, and has magic in it. Set it in the hilt of your sword for luck when you are man-grown – for you will be man-grown some day, in spite of the Clann Morna: and a good sword-thruster and a lavish-handed chieftain you will be!"

Fionn kept that sea-beast's tooth very carefully, and often when he went supperless to bed he repeated to himself the words of the swart-faced man – especially the words about a lavish-handed chieftain and good sword-thruster. He wished that he could come by a sword, but there seemed to be little chance of that. He made a sling for himself, and some sharp-pointed javelins; and with these he practiced till he could hit a mark at a good distance: it was generally a moving mark, for Fionn was a food-provider and came at last to outrun a deer and take a young boar single-handed.

One night a messenger burst from the shadows, panting and staggering like a spent hound. He spoke hurriedly with Bovemall, and slid into the forest without a word to Fionn.

When he had gone, Bovemall said:

"The end of our good days under the forest trees has come. Crimmall, your father's brother – he that held the broken clann together – is worsted in the game. He must seek a lair in the fastnesses of the west: there men starve in scant seasons, and live hardly at all times. But a worse thing is a-foot. The Clann Morna have knowledge of us. Uail's son lives, they know, and a forest shelters him. They have gathered many fierce dogs, and they will harry Ireland, forest by forest. Crimmall will be no longer here to withstand them or to send us news. It is upon the roadways of the world that we must travel now. It is among wayfarers and in the huts of churls that we must hide; and you must part from us, and lose yourself as comrade-boy to herd-boys, and boys that watch the sown field scattering the robber birds."

"I will be a hunter's lad," said Fionn, "or I will follow after fighting-men and learn their ways."

"Misery is a sharp teacher," said Bovemall, "and a bitter foster-mother: who knows if we shall ever sit together after to-night."

"Leave this guessing at fate," cried Liath. "You, Bovemall, have the druid wisdom, and the moon-bowl that makes wisdom known! Take it now and see what lies in wait for Fionn."

"When last I held that bowl between my hands and looked in it," said Bovemall, "I saw the death of Uail."

"After the red sun – the black faggots of night," said Liath, "after night – the ashes of dawn and the new-kindled sun! Take the bowl: ill-luck dies sometime, like everything else."

From a secret place Bovemall took a shallow bowl of pale gold. On the rim it was graven with ogham letters and figures of swans and dragons, but moon-pale and pure was the gold within. She filled the bowl with water. She recited the *rann* that gives vision; and sitting with the bowl between her hands, she said:

"Come hither, Fionn, White Blossom of my Heart, and move your right hand once above the water in the moon-bowl."

Fionn moved his right hand slowly above the water, then knelt by Bovemall. Liath also knelt. Bovemall looked steadily upon the pale gold water: and eager silence shut in all three of them for a space.

"Do you see aught?" asked Liath.

"I see Fionn in vision after vision, but they change too quickly: at times he is with other lads, at times alone, at times with a grim-faced churl, at times with a gentle poet – once with his mother! Now he is coming forward clearly. He is laughing, and many faces crowd behind him: faces of lads that are laughing and singing. O Fionn, I see you with sunshine on you and the gladness of victory. You are holding in your hands the Treasure-Wallet of Uail – you are holding it as Uail used to hold it for the Luck-Blessing!"

Bovemall rose and with a sudden gesture poured the water from the divining bowl on Fionn's head.

"*Hail,*" she cried, "*to the Luck-Bringer of Clann Bassna, Hail to the Bringer of the Treasure-Wallet!*"

Fionn did not quite know what was expected of him, so he kept silence: but Liath questioned Bovemall.

"Was it indeed The Treasure-Wallet, The Luck of the Clann, that he had?"

"It was indeed The Treasure-Wallet."

"Tell me of it," said Fionn, "never till this hour have you spoken of it."

"If your father had lived, you would have seen it ere this, for it was carried on festival days round the sacred flame. In it are the potent Talismans and the Jewels of Sovereignty that give luck to Clann Bassna; and supremacy to the Chieftain of the Clann."

"Where must I seek for it?" asked Fionn.

"It is with the worst traitor that ever reddened a hand in the blood of his lord."

"What name has he?" asked Fionn.

"He is Lia of Luachra, the man that had the right to guard the Treasure-Wallet, as his fathers before him had done. Greed to keep it came on him, and he trafficked with Goll of the Clann Morna to betray Uail for the bribe of that Wallet. He lied to Uail on the day of the battle of Cnucha saying that the Wallet was gone from him. The clann went to the combat without the luck-circling. Uail got his death: the strength of Clann Bassna was broken – and misfortune came to all of us!"

"You saw me with the Luck-Wallet," said Fionn.

"I saw you, Jewel of my Heart!"

"That means," said Fionn, "that I shall slay Lia of Luachra when strength comes to my hands."

"That means," said Bovemall, "that you will be Chieftain of Clann Bassna and Lord of the Fianna of Ireland." As she spoke a spark leaped from the fire and flamed for a moment in Fionn's deerskin tunic.

"Fire sends you a luck-spark like a true comrade," said Bovemall, "and see, the embers are turning to white ash. It is time for us to say the sleep-rann and to cover the red seed of the fire so that we can waken a spurt of flame in the greyness of dawn, for we must be a-foot and on our journey before the sun shakes the sleep-dews from his hair."

They said the sleep-rann then and covered the embers; and sound sleep held them through the night.

It was Bovemall who blew upon the embers till flame danced there; it was Bovemall who wakened Fionn, while Liath spread thin cakes of pounded acorn-meal to cook on the hot flag-stones and stored victuals for the journey in deerskin wallets. When they were ready to set forth, Bovemall said:

"It is for you, Fionn, to quench the embers for this last time and say farewell to the hearth-flame."

Carefully Fionn quenched the embers, then he strewed green boughs and leaves on them, and said:

"Sleep, Spirit of Flame,
With greenness and redness of blossom;
Do not gnaw upon the tree-roots
Or bite the grass-stems.
Sleep soundly, soundly, very soundly,
Till we, your friends, come – if ever we come – to waken you.
Sleep, Spirit of Flame."

Then Bovemall took wine and water and honey for a farewell gift to the forest that had sheltered them. When she poured the water, she said:

"Oak-wood that sheltered us, farewell! Sap be in your branches; fullness of acorns on your boughs. Health and plentiness of food to all your forest-children."

When she poured the wine, she said:

"*I pour wine for you, purple-red; overseas it came in oared galleys – foreign wine of the Greeks. May poets praise you and put jewel-names of you in well-hammered verse. May they make bruit of your loveliness in far-off haughty places, and in the walled cities of stranger-kings. Oak-wood that sheltered us, I pour wine for you.*"

When she poured the honey, she said:

"*I pour honey for you. Where honey is, there is the laughter and song of bees; and where mead is – the honey-brew – there is laughter of men; and song. Be laughter with you, laughter of sun and wind and running stream; and song of thrush and ousel and high soaring lark. My heart makes a song for you. Fionn is glad for you: and Ciath sings a druid song of peace. Oak-wood that sheltered us, farewell. Our hundred thousand blessings with you, and farewell.*"

So with that leave-taking they set out, each one going separately, on the highways of the world to brave what fortune might be-fall them.

THE SILVER POOL

Fionn walked sturdily forward. Birds were singing in leafy branches. The river Boyne showed a gleam of silver between tree-trunks; it made a soft plashing sound among its reeds. Fionn whistled a little tune as he walked. He had no plan in his mind, save to meet what happened: and day by day to grow tall and strong so that some day he might wrest the Treasure-Wallet from Lia of Luachra; avenge his father's wrong; and win to the headship of the Fianna. Many moons had withered in the sky since he had said farewell to Bovemall and Liath and the kindly oak forest. Many a buffet fate had dealt him since then: many a sharp and evil chance he had known; many a good happening. He had set eyes on many a hill, many a valley since then: he had seen many a proud chieftain's lime-washed dune. Sun had tanned him. His bright hair was cropped like the hair of a churl, chariot-dust of the roadway had grimed his deerskin tunic: save for the pride of his walk there was little to betray the chief's son in him.

The morning was hot, and the plashy sound of the Boyne drew Fionn to the riverside. Picking his way between alder and willow and flowering rush he came to where the water swirled in silvery singing reaches in the pool that is called the Pool of the Star-Dance. By the pool was a man in the garb of the fisher-folk drawing to land a small casting-net. There were silver-gleaming trout spotted with crimson in the net, but the man took them one by one and threw them into the pool again.

"Greeting to you," said Fionn, as he drew near, "and luck on your fishing."

"I have no luck on my fishing," said the man.

"It is a strange thing, indeed," said Fionn, "that you make naught of the red-spotted trout of the Boyne. There's few but yourself would grumble at so good a catch."

"One fish alone I am eager to snare," said the man, "and that is the purple-finned crimson-banded Salmon of Knowledge that has gold of the sun and silver of the moon in every scale of him."

"A wise woman taught me," said Fionn, "that the Salmon of Knowledge swims in the Heaven-World in the pool of the Sacred Hazels."

"She might have taught you, to boot," said the man, "that whatever happens in the Heaven-World makes a shadow of itself here. It is in this pool, they say, that the shadow-self of the Salmon of Knowledge swims. I would snare it."

"I have heard that men of learning and poets can snare the Salmon in a net made of their dreams," said Fionn, "and have thereafter one shining scale of him. You that are the Flower of Poets and the Jewel of Learning should have more than one scale."

"Why do you use this manner of speech to me, that am naught but a plain fisherman?"

"I know you for the King's Poet," said Fionn. "In the year of the Great Assembly I saw you riding on a white stallion with the mane and tail dyed purple; you were wearing the singing robe and the head-dress of a royal poet, and you had fifty princes in your train. I was crouching in the thickness of an oak-bough when you rode past the Wood of the Golden Hawks, and I thought that if I had choice of speech with any one man that went by me there in a flashing chariot, or on a proud-stepping horse, I would choose to have speech with you."

"What help is there in words?" said the man. "You could not teach me how to snare the Salmon: I could not teach you more wood-craft than you know already."

"You could teach me poetry," said Fionn; "and I could serve you: cut rushes for your bed; bring you eggs of the wild duck; and deer from the mountain, with swift hares of the valley."

"What learning and what arts and what weapon-knowledge have you come by?" asked the man.

"Sword-craft I had from a robber that forced me to consort with him. I herded cows for a herb-leech and learned the virtues of herbs. The ways of horses I learned among horse-boys. The forest taught me woodcraft; but he who is ignorant of poetry is but a churl!"

"You shall serve me," said the man, "what name have you? I am, as is known to you, Finnegas the Poet."

"Demna is my name," said Fionn, and in this he spake truth, for the name Fionn, which means Beautiful One, was a nickname.

So it came to pass that Fionn abode with the King's Poet. He plaited mats of rushes, he snared wild fowl, he culled water-cress and sweet and bitter herbs of the field such as go with savoury meats, he pounded acorns and made bread as he had seen Bovemall do in the forest. And the King's Poet talked with him of heroes and kings and of the art of verse and the ceremonial of palaces. Fionn stored these conversations in his mind: and always he practiced with his sling at casting stones, and with a sword of wood at thrusting and parrying, and with a pole cut from an ash tree he practiced the hurling of spears. He ran, and jumped, and wrestled with tough boughs and saplings, so that he might grow in strength and hardihood. He put words together in praise of forest things and in praise of the small blossoms of the field and the songs of the blackbird and thrush: the King's Poet taught him how to shape them till he could make good well-hammered verse.

On a day of the days it chanced that Fionn had been praised for a poem, and in lightness of heart he set off to search for eggs of the plover that are delicate to the taste, for he had in mind to make festival for the King's Poet: that had naught himself in mind but the swirling of the Boyne and the Salmon that might lurk in the shallows, or in deep melodious reaches of the waters.

Fionn got the eggs and turned homeward. As he went, his foot struck on something hard, and stooping he saw a piece of strangely shaped greenish metal that had thrust from the marsh-soil. There was something familiar in the curve of it, and his hands dug eagerly into the grass-roots; more and more eagerly as the treasure unbared itself. At last he drew it forth – a bronze sword, double-edged and perfect! A sword that Gobniu the Smith might have fashioned: a sword that Lugh might have reddened in the battle of Moytura. Fionn rubbed it with a bunch of grass till it shone greenly, he fingered the finely tapered edges, he gripped the hilt: and all the while the tears ran down his face.

"My Treasure," he cried, "if Uail could see you; or Bovemall that had no sword to give me! If Crimmall knew I had you, his heart would be glad. I will show you to the sunlight. I will take you where you can hear loud battle-shouts – loud as those you heard before the man that had you flung from him lest his slayers should boast of you! Flame of Battle be glad of me – be glad of me!"

Fionn leaped to his feet, flung the sword into the air, caught it midway and whirled it about his head. Then he gathered up his plover eggs and set off at a run.

As he neared the pool where the King's Poet fished, day in and day out, he saw that something must have happened. The King's Poet was coming hastily to him gesticulating and shouting. Fionn hurried a little more and caught the words.

"I have snared him! I have snared him," the King's Poet was shouting, "I have snared the Salmon of Knowledge!"

And sure enough a small salmon, all silver-scaled and blue and carmine spotted, lay glinting on the bank.

"By what token do you know it for the Salmon of Knowledge," asked Fionn.

"Never have I snared the like of it," said the King's Poet, "and there is a prophecy that the Salmon of Knowledge will be snared in this pool, and eaten by a poet named Finnegas or Fionn. Now I am Finnegas and I will eat this Salmon."

"Indeed you shall eat it with heartiness and enjoyment," said Fionn, "and I will broil it for you as Bovemall taught me to broil the salmon of the Shannon that are kings' food. I have plover eggs too, and sharptasting herbs: sweet and bitter."

"I will touch naught but the Salmon, that I may have wisdom through it," said Finnegas.

Fionn made ready an oven and broiled the Salmon: but sitting by it, his mind wandered to the sword, and a flame licked the salmon-scales. Fionn turned the fish hastily and as he did so, a little bit of scale stuck to his thumb and burned him. He thrust his thumb into his mouth without thinking and so tasted the Salmon. He watched his work carefully after that, and when the fish was cooked through and through he brought it to Finnegas. Finnegas prepared to eat it as one should eat a sacred fish.

Fionn sat by the riverbank and his thoughts were on his sword. Suddenly he was aware that the King's Poet stood beside him.

"A strange thing has happened, Demna," said the Poet, "the savour and virtue of the Salmon have gone. It is as any other fish. Can it be that you have tricked me and have eaten of it?"

"Nay," said Fionn, "I have not tasted of it, save for a scale that clung, burning, to my thumb."

"That scale has taken the virtue of the fish," said the Poet, "and yet it is strange that a prophecy could be so easily broken. The Salmon was for a poet called Fionn, or Finnegas – and you are Demna!"

"Demna is my name, but I am called Fionn: it is a nick-name that stuck to me."

"Fionn, henceforth, will be your true name: for now I see that the Salmon was meant for you. It is not to one who is weary of mart and court and battleground that the Salmon of Knowledge will give himself, but to one who is eager for the sword-hilt and amorous of life."

"I have a sword," cried Fionn. "A sword for a king it is! A luck-bringer, a battle-queller, a singer of war-songs!" He held up the sword, his eyes caressing it.

Finnegas took it in his hands.

"May luck be with it," he said, "it is indeed a royal sword. How came you by it?"

Fionn told the story of its finding.

"Some Lord of the Shining Folk has blessed this day for you," said Finnegas. "Salmon and Sword! What have you in mind to do with your fortune?"

"I have in mind to avenge my father that was treacherously slain."

"What man was your father? "asked Finnegas, "I know well you are no churl's son."

"I would name my father," said Fionn, "only to one that had loved him, or to the High King of Ireland on that day when I win back my heritage. I am no churl's son, Finnegas, and if I live I will set poetry as a craft for warriors. I will come, too – if I win out – to seek you in whatever place you may be!"

"I know not in what place I may be," said Finnegas, "mayhap at Tara with the High King; mayhap in some mountain wilderness; mayhap in this hut by the river, if I be not under the sod – but tell me what way of life do you plan for yourself: for I know you will not tarry with me longer."

"I purpose to join with myself other lads, as I find them," said Fionn, "and practice feats and stratagems till we can make ourselves felt in some foray and come by weapons: then we will seek a warrior that is kin to me – outlawed now and in hiding – and do as his wisdom counsels."

"I dare predict that you will win your heritage," said the King's poet.

"Eat now the Salmon, and we will spend the hours that remain to us in the telling of tales and the recital of poems and in sound sleep: that to-morrow may be fortunate for your setting forth."

So Fionn ate the Salmon, and wondered if its wisdom would help him to find lads like himself, eager to venture; comrades of the Sword and the Treasure-Wallet. And the King's poet ate the plover eggs with the sweet and bitter herbs; and wondered whether it would be wise to go back again to the bright-coloured loud-sounding life of palaces; or wiser to stay in the little hut by the Boyne, watching cloud-shadows: and herons brooding on reedy pools.

THE LORDSHIP OF THE FIANNA

THE ROAD TO TARA

Fionn, son of Uail, stood on a small eminence and let his eyes delight themselves with the palaces of Tara. They were spread multitudinously below him, with their silken banners and their carved roof-poles and their gaily coloured walls, like a piece of rich broidery-work flung for a vaunt on the green slanting meadows. Fionn had dreamed of those palaces upon hearsay for many a long year. His childish mind had coloured them and carved their roof beams with incredible devices. Man-grown his desire had dwelt among them. He had toughened his sinews in many a fight, he had endured hardship, he had denied himself pleasure, for the sake of this moment – Tara beneath him, and his feet on the road to it! The sun was high in the heavens, he had no need to hasten his steps. The palaces of Conn, Son of Felimy, the king that his father had loved; the palaces where Goll could lord it now as chief of the Fianna of Ireland! Uail, while he lived had been chief of the Fianna: Goll had slain him.

"It is a goodly spectacle," said a voice beside him, "fill your eyes with it. To-morrow the sun will look on blackened ruins."

"Who are you," cried Fionn, "to prophesy such a devastation?"

"I am Datho, one who has lands and thralls in this place. If you were not country-bred and a stranger you would know that on the Eve of Sowan, every three years, Allyn, son of Midna, burns Tara."

"One man burns Tara!"

"He is of the Folk of Dahna: and those that are wise in such matters say even that he comes from the Mountain of the Smith, Slieve Cullion."

"The Mountain of Cullion! The Mountain of Mananaun?"

"That Mountain! And it is from Shee Finnacha where Lear himself dwells that he comes: the High Radiant Dwelling-Place on the crest of the Mountain that is crowned with Flames redder than carbuncle stones through the hours of the day; and crowned with White Fire at night, lest man or beast or smallest creeping thing set foot there."

"Have not the Gods their share of honour?" asked Fionn, "Have they not their fill of praise and sacrifice? Why does this one torment us?"

"If the ancient rocks know it they keep the secret: but men will never be without stories of any happenings; or deaf to prophecies and haphazard sayings."

"What stories have they of this happening?"

"They say it is for the sake of a spear. They say that Uail, he that was chief of Clann Bassna and Head of the Fianna once, took that spear out of a Faery Palace, the palace of Allyn, son of Midna."

"Where is that spear?" cried Fionn.

"Where is last year's snow?" said the man.

"Is it with Goll of the Clann Morna the spear is?"

"It is not with Goll, or with any man so far as is known. Goll sacked the strong dune of Uail and took many a treasure from it, but he did not take the spear."

"Has strength withered in the hand of every champion: is there no strength in the battalions of the Fianna to withstand the burning?"

"You can try your own strength on it for the matter of that," said Datho. "The king offers his choice of a reward, and the contentment of his heart-wish, to the man who will stay the burning."

"Has Goll made trial of it?"

"Aye, Goll has made trial of it; and Goll's brother Garra; and bald-headed Cunnaun: the king himself has made trial; and slept with the best of them!"

"Slept!"

"Even so – slept – for when Allyn, son of Midna, comes he brings such music with him that a man in the very extremity of torture would sleep at the sound of it. The hounds sleep, the very rats in the granaries sleep. Everything that draws the breath of life sleeps, till Allyn, son of Midna, makes an end of playing. It is music he brings instead of a sword."

"If Uail, son of Trenmor, were here there might be need of a sword."

"Uail did not keep his own head safe," said Datho, "upon his proud shoulders."

"Who are you to take lightly in your mouth the name of Uail, son of Trenmor, son of Bassna?"

"One that saw him in his magnificence a time or two: but if you would speak with a clansman that held him dear from boyhood, there limps your choice!"

A large-limbed man, whom age had bowed without taming, was walking heavily and lamely along the road. He carried three freshly caught trout on a gad.

"That man," said Datho, "is Fiacha, son of Conga, once a man of mark, a follower that wrecked his fortunes for Uail. Rather than submit to Goll he lives in a mean hut without even a hound to share his poverty."

"I will speak with him," said Fionn.

"Come hither, Fiacha, son of Conga," cried Datho, "here is one that would question you."

"I am beholden to no man," said Fiacha, "let him who would question me keep step for step with me on the road."

"Well-spoken!" cried Fionn, and crossing to the old man he kept step for step with him on the road.

"What name do you bear," asked Fiacha, "you who would question me?"

"I am Fionn, son of Uail, son of Trenmor, son of Bassna."

The old man stopped suddenly on the road: his hands began to tremble.

"Why do you say this thing to tempt me?" he cried.

"I say the truth to you: have I no semblance of my father?"

The old man peered closely into Fionn's face. "You have Uail's eyes," he said, "and if you be indeed his son, tell me what mark was on the Treasure-Wallet of Uail."

"The Treasure-Wallet came from the Brugh of Angus: the marks that are upon the threshold stone of the Brugh are upon the Treasure-Wallet."

"Oh, if your hands have touched it, tell me how is it marked within."

"It is marked within with the secret names of the Four jewels that the Gods of Dahna brought from the Heaven World."

"May the sun protect you, Fionn son of Uail: may the earth make safe the pathways for you. Have you, my lord, the Treasure-Wallet of Uail?"

"I have the Treasure-Wallet."

"Pulse of my Heart, and Chieftain of Clann Bassna, I have a gift for you," said Fiacha, "poor and broken though I am – I have a thing hidden away; a treasure that I never hoped to put in the hand of Uail's son."

"Good will be the gift of one who loved my father. Tell me of it."

"It is the Spear that Uail took from the Gods of Dahna. I snatched it away, wrapped in its cloak of darkness, even whilst Goll and his people sacked the dune. Wrapped in its cloak I buried it, and over the place of its sepulchre I built my poor hut. To-night, if you will, your hands shall hold it."

"Fiacha, friend of my father, with that Spear to-night I may win back my heritage: for it is in my mind to try fortunes with Allyn son of Midna."

"Terrible is the Spear, son of Uail. I would not bribe you with it to your death. Who knows if Allyn can be slain!"

"My mind was hardened to encounter him ere I met you. With or without the Spear I will engage to guard Tara to-night."

"The word in your mouth is the word of a chief. Hasten to Tara. Say naught of the Spear. I will bring it to you secretly when you shall have chosen your vantage ground."

"Fiacha," said Fionn, "had my father lived he would have given me to a princely house to foster. I have a noble foster-mother though she fostered me without a roof. No man is my foster-father: if I win out to-night, I will be your foster-son."

"Win victory, son of Uail! I would say that to you though you should never waste a second word on me. Win victory for Uail that is dead, and for the broken men of the Clann Bassna."

"For Clann Bassna!" said Fionn, and he set forth swiftly on the road to Tara.

CONN THE HUNDRED-FIGHTER

Conn the Hundred-Fighter sat in his chair of state in the royal hall at Tara. A tower of strength was Conn the Hundred-Fighter, a flaming torch of valour, a candle of munificence. Gorgeously apparelled he made a brightness where he sat. The Chief Druid, Kith the Red, was on his right, his head bound with a golden fillet, his purple robe embroidered in seven colours: on his left was the Royal Poet wearing his ceremonial robe made of the bright feathers of birds. Huge waxen candles lit the hall, their reflections danced and flickered on the walls where thin sheets of beaten copper took the place of tapestry. Riveted with studs and knobs of red bronze that copper was, and fashioned to the shapes of strange birds; birds such as druids summon with incantations. Upon the crests of these birds jewels glittered, cunningly wrought: red carbuncles served them for eyes.

There was gloom on the face of Conn: his brows were drawn in a frown, his thoughts were on the burning of Tara. And even as he sat thus, the trumpets of his proclamation sounded without. Great trumpets of bronze, brazen-throated, of a bulk that scarce one man could carry; they made a roaring sound like the bellowing of unearthly bulls or like thunder shut in a cavern. Seven of them gave bellowing voice, and earth reverberated with the sound. Scarce had the air ceased to tremble when Conn seized the bell-branch, the branch of silver with little bells upon it like apples of gold. Conn shook it for silence within the hall; it made a high sweet ecstatic sound like the twittering of small birds in springtime. The loud voice of the herald came resonant from without:

"The High King of Ireland, Conn the Hundred Fighter, offers to whatsoever warrior, magician, son of learning, Poet, or simple artificer, has power or skill to keep the flames this night from Tara, his own asking of reward: and the contentment of his heart's wish if it be in a king's power to grant it."

The trumpets bellowed again: and whilst they bellowed, Fionn entered the hall. His red-gold hair and his height would have drawn men's eyes in any assembly. Tall and lithe and strong he was and young and goodly to look upon: his hair was wound close about his head, braided like the locks of a champion ready for combat, but save for the short sword in his belt he had neither shield nor weapon.

"Greeting to the High King of Ireland," said Fionn, "may prosperity multiply itself upon him."

"Greeting and blessing to you, young warrior," replied Conn.

"High King of Ireland," said Fionn, "if it should please the Gods that I shelter Tara from the flames to-night, will you indeed give me my own asking of a reward: and my heart's desire to me?"

"I will give it indeed," said the King.

Fionn looked to where Goll sat, broad-shouldered and fierce-eyed under his thick brows.

"O King," said Fionn, "it may be that to some lords in this assembly the reward I have it in my mind to ask will prove unpleasing. I would have the King's word bound on sureties."

Conn laughed a great laugh and looked round his hall. Kings from the five provinces of Ireland were there; they had come to take part in the ceremonies of the Festival of Sowan; magicians and druids of note were there.

"You have a high and confident heart, my Champion," said Conn, "will you bind the bond on the kings that are here; and on Red Kith, the chief magician; and the magicians that follow him?"

"I could ask no better sureties," said Fionn.

Then was the oath tied with magic knots and strength of earth and fire and water to the satisfaction of Fionn. It was an uplifting of heart to the assembly.

"Tell me, my Treasure," said Conn, "of what lineage are you, and what name had your father?"

"Royal King," said Fionn, "I have not uttered my father's name save in secret: let it still be secret if I perish to-night. If I win victory I will make known my father's name and his lineage when I ask my reward."

"Let it be so, my Hawk of Battle," said the King, "and if shield or spear be lacking to you, choose from the best of mine."

"I have proffer of a weapon," said Fionn, "it will suffice me."

"May the great Battle-Queen lend power to it," said the King, "and drink now a horn of mead with me and with these kings and lords who wish you well."

The cupbearers of the king filled a horn of white bronze. Fionn took it in his hand.

"Win victory and blessing, O King," he said, "this hour, and in every hour that the Smith hammers out for you."

"Win victory and blessing, my Hawk of Battle," said the King.

Fionn turned himself to the gathering night.

THE SPEAR BIRGHA

Behind Fionn, ramparted Tara crouched in darkness. The King had ordered it so. No smallest glimmer of a rushlight showed in any place: if Tara flamed to-night it would be lit by Allyn, son of Midna. From the North the son of Midna would come: even now he might be approaching, and Fionn had not the Spear! Alert as a wolf, his eyes searched the gloom, his ears searched the stillness; and before he could see anything he knew by faint and scarce detected sounds that someone was coming with stealthy cautious steps.

"Son of Uail," a voice whispered, "it is I, Fiacha, I have the Spear."

"My blessing on you," said Fionn, "give it into my hands; it is my choice of a weapon to-night."

"Very terrible is the Spear," said Fiacha, "Birgha it is named: feel how the blade leaps and quivers, even though the cloak that is wound so tightly all the length of it blinds and restrains it. A demon writhes there: only once did your father unhood it, and then – by a hazard leap from his hand – it drank the life-blood of a warrior that he loved!"

Fionn's eager fingers closed on the haft: his hand moved circumspectly on the muffled blade.

"It lives, of a truth," he said, "but this cloak that hoods it seems no more than a silken swathe."

"Do not unwind that swathe till you are ready to launch the Spear. It is a cloak of some outlandish stuff: so fine that you could draw it through your thumb-ring. It came from that same palace whence your father reft the Spear: the ardency of the blade has not worn it, nor the years of its hiding cankered it. I would you could see the colours it has. It is a cloak from Faeryland."

"My mother came thence; mayhap she had such cloaks."

"Do not tangle your mind with aught but the night's work," said Fiacha. "If sleep does not thicken my lids, my heart will watch with you."

"Your heart will watch," said Fionn, "and dead men that were comrades of yours may watch in company. Go safely!"

"Win victory and blessing, Son of Uail: and should this night thrust you from life, say to Uail that Fiacha, Conga's son, was faithful."

Fionn was alone. The Spear writhed and trembled in his grasp. The dark plain spread widely to the dark horizon. It was Sowan Eve: no one who could help it would be outdoors on Sowan Eve. Every palisaded dune, every wattled hut would be closed and barred tonight. But the dunes of the Folk of Dahna would be open. The mountain-palaces would be open. To-night the Folk of Dahna walked abroad. To-night they had power. To-night, if a man dared the hazard, he could question the gods! Fionn tightened his grasp on the Spear: he was glad to feel the demon life in it, glad to feel it writhe and twist in his hands, eager and venomous.

The night crawled dumbly by like a wounded cumbrous beast dragging its heavy length. Fionn's mind dragged wearily and heavily like the hours; his hands wrestled with the Spear. No sight – no sound – no faintest stirring! So the hours dragged: endlessly, listlessly. But of a sudden between his hands the Spear tensed. The earth stirred itself. The air took lightness. MUSIC! Yes, it was music, very far off: a faint music, yet shrill and of an unearthly sweetness.

Fionn never could say afterwards what instrument it was that played. It was like a high lilting voice, and at the sound of it something in himself gave a great leap for joy: he felt that he was towering above himself, towering as if to equal the surge of melody, the tumult that was suddenly everywhere: in the earth; in the air; in the low distant hills; in the near-by dark druid-hill of Thlacta. Voices cried in that mighty surge; exultantly, defiantly: voices piercing sweet, in a monotony of one note; harsh voices that wavered like tongues of flame. Vast litanies intoned themselves with multitudinous responses as if every forest leaf had a tongue. Trumpets gave it urgency. There were clashings of cymbals: and sweet strings of viol; and timpaun; and harp. Voices more than mortal sang in exalted chorus: and through every maze of sound there ran and scintillated and glittered-like stars in the milky way, like sparks of fire from an anvil – a myriad silver tinklings of shaken bells.

Minute by minute the music changed. It was patterned, as reedy shallows are patterned by the feet of the wind: it gathered itself as a wave gathers, curving to fall: and like foam on the running eager crest of a wave – like the silvery flash of a salmon in swirling waters – the first unearthly melody, the high lilting sweetness, maintained itself. Ah, what was it that the son of Midna was playing? Why did Fionn take part with him against himself? He was playing the stars out of the sky; he was playing the earth to nothingness, and yet Fionn exulted and towered out of his body to listen! What was that thin sweet song! Sun moon and stars were dust upon the wind – small scattered dust – and yet the song persisted: how could so thin and fine a sweetness consume the heart?

It was Fionn's heart now that fed the song, it was his strength that shrivelled in the wind: almost fainting he leant his forehead on the spear-point. And then he knew a strange thing. The Spear Birgha had a song – a song like a shaft of white light! Birgha, the Spear, was singing of battles, and of hero-deeds; of hazards and ventures; and of hardship; of men that dared, and snatched a victory; of men that dared, and lost: and recked not of loss. What vibrant strength was in the song! Fionn's heart grew red again and his feet took a firmer grip of the Earth.

But was it the Earth – any Earth that Fionn knew? The grass was taking colour of greenness – burning with greenness such as never daylight gave it! Flowers of scarlet and vermilion and azure – flowers the sun had never looked upon – trembled in it. The great dome of the sky bent low and low, a burning insufferable sapphire.

And now he saw the son of Midna, as if he had stepped over the rim of the world. Every colour flamed and flashed about him, every surge of melody pulsed and fell: the whiteness of his body in the midst of it was like the whiteness of flame.

Fionn thrust the point of the Spear savagely against his forehead. He was standing for the men of Clann Bassna: men who had watched and starved on the hills; who had died in waste places, fugitive and broken – men who had kept the will to thwart Destiny. Hunted, harassed, poverty-bitten, they were outcast for Uail his father; they had died – some of them – for Fionn. They were blood of his blood; bone of his bone. Did they not cry to him out of their anguish, out of their unvanquishable valour: "Stand fast. STAND FAST."

Fionn began to unswathe the Spear: with deliberation he unswathed it lest he should injure the cloak; and as he loosened it, Allyn son of Midna – blinding, terrible in his beauty – was close upon him. He stood for a moment like a bright unearthly bird. He did not seem to be aware of Fionn, his eyes looked through and beyond Fionn as though he looked into the nothingness that is beyond the world.

He blew a breath from between his lips towards the ramparted palaces of Tara.

The hissing fierceness of lightning was in that breath!

Fionn had but loosed the cloak: almost despairingly he held it spread against that vehemence of flame. The flame played upon the cloak, dazzling it to a thousand colours: then sped hissing into the earth.

Allyn son of Midna blew for the second time a breath from between his lips towards the ramparted palaces of Tara.

It had the white fierceness of lightning – that breath! Like lightning it shone and dazzled on the cloak; and sped hissing into the earth.

Allyn son of Midna cast a glance about him as a mighty antlered stag casts a glance when he is aware of some forest portent and scarce knows whether to fight or flee.

A third time he blew a breath towards the ramparted palaces of Tara.

A third time the vehement hissing flame descended into the earth!

Then Allyn son of Midna turned and fled.

With the naked Spear in his grasp Fionn son of Uail leaped after him: and still the music surged; and still the voices cried in it; still every instrument made riotous ecstasy while reeling earth and reeling heaven flamed together! Fionn could be sure of naught in this strange world save the beating of his heart and the pounding of his feet as he ran. Light as flame ran Allyn son of Midna; and behind him and about him and before him the earth blossomed in starry fire.

Northward they sped – northward towards the Mountain of the Smith, towards the Radiant Dwelling Place, Shee Finnaclaa.

Splashing through the shallows of the Boyne, Fionn lifted a handful of the silvery sacred water and dashed it in his face and eyes. "Hail Goddess," he cried in a choking salutation, for the river was sacred to Dahna, the Mighty Mother. It may be that she helped him: it may be that the son of Midna felt the strangeness of Fionn's world clogging and interpenetrating his own, for he ran with less lightness. And Fionn, running like a wolf – the beast that brings down every other by sheer persistency – felt strength and toughness increasing in himself.

So they sped northward – always northward.

Allyn son of Midna was no longer aurioled. The music too was swooning to a stillness. Fionn heartened himself – and heartened himself again. The son of Midna was naught but a slender youth running wearily. Yet he could not come within spear-cast!

It was so till Slieve Cullion – the Mountain of the Smith, the Hammerer, the Shaper and Fashioner of the World – stood in their path. Fionn knew that mountain shouldering against the sky, steep and shaggy. Allyn son of Midna could not breast it, running so wearily. Fionn heartened himself once more – yet the son of Midna kept out of spear-cast! Then, of a sudden the mountain opened. It was not a mountain but a fortressed dune, a great palace whose roofs and pinnacles glittered to the stars and lost themselves amongst them!

Mountain-vast within, the palace glowed with a soft and changing radiance and from the deep recesses of its portal the Folk of Dahna like bright-coloured blossoms looked out. They cried encouragement to Allyn son of Midna: yet ever he ran more wearily, lagging step by step. Fionn – running as the wolf runs on the track of a hind – judged his distance. Suddenly with all his force he loosed the Spear, Birgha. It struck the son of Midna between the shoulders and pierced him through. At that the Folk of Dahna gave a great anguished cry: but the son of Midna by a mighty effort kept his feet. Lagging, fainting, he stumbled on.

"Win victory, O Blossomed Branch, win victory," cried the folk in the portal: but they did not leave the shelter of the dune; they did not stretch rescuing hands to the son of Midna. Almost as his feet gained the threshold Fionn seized him by the hair and drew him backward – drew him reeling to the earth!

With his fall there came a sound like a clap of thunder. The air was full of voices that cried: "*Aie*," "*Aie*", "*Aie*", but there was no glimmer of radiance left, nor any pinnacle of all that heaven-scaling host. In a cold pallor of waning stars Slieve Cullion shouldered the sky blackly.

In the thin cold light of stars Fionn looked down upon his capture. Allyn son of Midna lay as one dead: yet his body – pallid and slender, white as the shadow of the moon in water – showed no wound! Fionn's eyes searched for the Spear: keen as a hawk questing the ground, he searched for the Spear, Birgha. It was nowhere – nowhere! Fionn's gaze came back to the son of Midna: he was loath to draw weapon upon that fairness; his hands were loath to touch again hair that kept such brightness.

The son of Midna leaned upwards on one arm. He smiled wearily and mockingly at Fionn, his eyelids heavy on his eyes.

"My head is yours," he said, "for a night and part of a day. The Spear is mine till the end of time. I do not rue the bargain."

He let himself sink back upon the earth: he shuttered his eyes; and neither spoke word after that; nor drew breath.

Fionn took his head.

TARA

The nobles of Tara, at the palace gates, spread their cloaks for Fionn to tread upon; and cried:

"Let the Saviour of Tara give battle-luck!"

And so he came proudly before the King.

"Conn the Hundred-Fighter, son of Felimy, High King of Ireland," he said, "I bring you the head of Allyn son of Midna: grant to me my heart's desire, and my own asking of reward. It is Fionn, son of Uail, son of Trenmor, son of Bassna, who asks."

There was clash and rumour of voices in the hall: and chiefs got to their feet. 'Fionn son of Uail! Son of Trenmor!' Some whispered it in consternation, some doubtfully; some with open joy. 'Son of Uail' – that name ran through the assembly – son of the great dead chief! Fionn, the Saviour of Tara!'

Conn the Hundred-Fighter shook the bell-branch till there was a great silence in the hall.

"Set the head of him that blackened Tara, pole-high upon the ramparts that the sun may look scornfully upon it; and the eyes of the people behold it," said the King, "and give ear to the Champion who has brought deliverance."

In all that assembly there was not one who did not turn his eyes upon Fionn.

"Son of Uail, what is your request," said Conn the Hundred-Fighter, "and what is the fulfilment of your heart's desire?"

"I ask the Lordship of the Fianna of Ireland," said Fionn, "and recompense and honour and the favour of the King's countenance for the broken men of Clann Bassna: that is my heart's desire."

"The Lordship of the Fianna, you have won," said the King, "and favour and recompense and honour for the men of Clann Bassna: and here before the kings and poets and royal druids shall the chiefs and leaders and champions of the Fianna swear faith to you. And if there is one who withholds service from you, let him take ship for Alba or for Scotland or whatever country seems good to him on the ridge of the world, and depart thence."

Goll, son of Morna – lord, till that moment, of the Fianna of Ireland – got to his feet.

"Fionn, son of Uail," he said, "Your battle-skill outbids mine. I put my hand in yours: I am your man."

Goll's brothers, Garra and Cunnaun and Art, and the chiefs next in rank to them, stood up and spoke as Goll had spoken: and with oaths and fitting ceremonies their fealty was bound to Fionn. But as they greeted him with joyous acclamation there rose a great clangour and clamour without, and one entered the hall crying:

"Behold a marvel – a marvel, O King! Scarce had we set the head of Allyn son of Midna high upon the rampart pole – that all the folk might look on it – scarce had the sun beheld it, when a great bird swooped sudden out of the sky. Feathered with silver and crested with gold that bird was. He stooped upon the rampart-pole, he cherished and sheltered the head – there with his feathers, and rising bore it away: making a sweet and lamentable crying."

"It is well known to us," said the King, "that Allyn son of Midna was of the Folk of Dahna. They care for their own."

But Fionn turned over in his mind the son of Midna's words:

'My head is yours for a night, and part of a day. The Spear is mine till the end of time. I do not rue the bargain.'

THE TANGLE-COATED HORSE

The sun was yellowing towards evening. Fionn, Son of Uail, chief of the warriors and hunters of Ireland, sat on a hillside that had the greenness of Spring. Close by him sat Bran, the hound that could bring down a stag single-handed, and at his feet stretched the shaggy hound, Lomair, and the shaggier hound, Sgeolaun. All about the hillside were Fionn's men, building ovens and setting deer-meat and boar-flesh on spits for roasting.

Diarmid the Brown-Haired, young and slender, lay idle as a flower on the grass, and at his side sprawled big bald-headed, heavy-girthed Cunnaun.

"I am the man," Cunnaun was saying, "that knows the points of a horse. That is sure – as sure a thing as that Fionn's men are called the Fianna of Ireland! I could pick a horse from one hundred horses with one glance of my eye."

"You could," said Diarmid, "and a choice horse he would be – a big-boned slow-mover that plants himself in the earth every time he sets a foot down: a horse with a back so broad you couldn't topple off him if you tried, Cunnaun. I could make a song about the kind of horse that you would pick:

"*A horse so nice*
You kick him twice
Before he moves.
A horse with hooves
Like water-vats.
He has an ear that flops
A high back-bone that drops
A tail for switching flies
He can't run when he tries,
Bald Cunnaun's horse."

"You think yourself clever, Diarmid the Brown-Haired," said Cunnaun, "because you're long-legged and lath-like and a good runner, but the brown hare goes quicker for his size and the daddy-long-legs is more slender of body than you are. I was slender of body myself when I was your age, and as for horses —"

"As for horses," said Diarmid,

"*If a horse you want*
To sweat and pant
To jib and veer
When work's to do,
To rear and hoyse

Just pick the choice
Of Cunnaun here
You'll never rue
Bald Cunnaun's choice."

Diarmid chanted this ditty in a high lilting voice and at the end of it he neighed like a horse. A high screaming unearthly terrible neigh answered him. It was as if a hundred horses neighed with one ghostly voice. Diarmid jumped to his feet, Cunnaun lumbered up, every head on the hillside craned in one direction. Coming towards them was a big shambling loose-jointed tangle-coated horse: and walking step for step with him was a big shambling loose-jointed tangle-headed man. Every time the man put a big flat foot down, the earth shook: and every time the horse put a big flat foot down, the earth shook a lot more.

"Don't hurry yourself, my Jewel," said the big man to the horse, "we must have a shape of comeliness on ourselves when the great chief, Fionn, the son of Uail, sets eyes on us."

"Who are you to have the name of Fionn, the son of Uail, in your mouth," cried Cunnaun, "speaking it in the hairy villainous ear of a brute that's your blood-cousin in ugliness!"

"Keep the rough edge of your tongue off my horse, bald man," said the stranger. "If he took notice of you at all he would think you too big for one bite and too little for two: if he raised one foot to you, you wouldn't stop spinning through the air till you landed like a wisp of nothingness in a country that you never heard the name of even!"

"Go your ways to Fionn," said Cunnaun, "you and your brute."

Forward trampled that horse and man to where Fionn was sitting, and Cunnaun and Diarmid moved themselves into ear-shot; so did everyone else.

"Fionn, son of Uail," said the big man, "it is noised about the edges of the world that never yet have you put refusal on prince or churl that came a-begging to you for a meal's meat and a day's work. I am asking you to give myself and my horse here, a meal's meat and a day's work."

"What work can you do?" asked Fionn.

"I am not skilled or unskilled in work. I have but one gift to make-vaunt-of: I am the laziest serving-man in the whole wide world! If you searched through all the sea-depths, you could not find a lazier; if you reached your hand to the sky, you could not pluck a lazier out of it. That is the one gift I have, Fionn."

"Mayhap," said Fionn, "your horse does work for two."

"Work is it? There's many a foolishness that horse has, as close to him as his own bones, but the foolishness of work he never had – and I never urged it upon him, for think now: a man might be blossomed in silver and fruited in gold but what's that to him if he has a kitthogue of a wife, and what source of delight would it be to my Treasure here to have the laziest master in the world if he weren't free himself to keep the moon of midnight and the sun of noon-day dancing to the whimsies of his mind?"

The horse leered and winked at his master with one of his yellow vicious eyes, and his long yellow teeth made a snap at the head of the nearest of Fionn's men. The man leaped aside just in time.

"It will task me," said Fionn, "to measure a day's work for you and your companion, but a meal's meat I can give you without stint."

"O Fionn," said the big man, "may your shadow never grow less; may you have kine knee-deep in a thousand meadows; may all the bees in Ireland gather honey for your mead-vats, for it is you that will be acclaimed the Candle of Generosity when I and my Treasure have eaten a meal's meat!"

"I'll warrant me," cried Cunnaun, "that you can eat all before you as the darkness eats a hillside – and be the leaner for it! From cavernous emptiness comes loud-mouthed boasting."

The big man turned to his horse. "Shut fast your ears, O incomparable One," he said, "shut fast your ears against the niggard words of this man. He would begrudge you the dewdrop on a blade of grass, and you wouldn't get a mouthful the size of a spider's foothold if he had the giving of it, but turn yourself to Fionn here that is the Torch and Noon-Day Sun of Munificence."

The yellow-coated horse swung round and lowered his head before Fionn till his nose touched the earth; then he made a leap into the air, spread all his four big-hooved feet in a kick that went every way at once, and somersaulted and catapulted and buck-jumped towards a green hollow place of young sweet spring grass. Cunnaun's horses were in that hollow place, and almost before he could clap palms together or let cry one "Ochone!" that horse was on them like a thunderbolt and all about him was a biting, kicking, swirling whirlwind of hair and hooves and flashing teeth. Cunnaun spun hither and thither like a leaf in a storm, waving his arms and shouting:

"Ochone! Ochone! My horses! My horses! Call your lean-ribbed brute out of my pasture: call him, or I'll break every bone in his body!"

"Call him out, yourself, bald Cunnaun. My mind is filled with the thought of oxen roasted whole and wild boars stuffed with garlic and haunches of venison and vats of mead: not for a trifle would I roughen my tongue that is honeyed now with expectation. Your tongue is edged, Cunnaun. Call him, yourself."

Cunnaun seized a boar-spear and hurled himself down the hill-slope. Soon he was thrusting terribly at the tangle-coated horse: thrusts that should have been gashes and deathly wounds to him, but the point slid off and left the beast unhurt – not a thrust of them all knocked a hair out of his hide! Cunnaun gathered his strength for one mighty thrust. The spear-point slid from that shaggy shoulder and glanced along the bony ribs: it did not even leave a scratch there! It just seemed to tickle the yellow horse, for he stopped snapping and kicking and turned round to look at Cunnaun. He winked at him first with one eye and then he winked with the other eye and all the while he smiled, and smiled, and smiled, till his face was nothing but a smile. Cunnaun hit him one last resounding smack, and the boar-spear fell in two halves.

"It's a demon he is," cried Cunnaun, "or a dragon maybe from under the sea, or a piast that tried to put the shape of a horse on himself! O the black hour of misfortune that brought him on us and we with no thought at all of the like of him. He'll eat Fionn out of house and home! O my grief and my sorrow for the boar-spear, the good trusty boar-spear that I've splintered on him!"

"Try kindness," said Diarmid, "and honeyed words: there is great power in honeyed words."

"Try them yourself," said Cunnaun.

"I will," said Diarmid, and with that he vaulted on the back of the horse and took a hard twisted grip of the mane. The horse winked with both eyes together at Diarmid, and Diarmid kicked him with his heels.

"Come," he said, "put one foot before the other, and I will take you where you can eat your fill."

But the horse stood still as a stone.

"Young chief," said the big man, coming up. "Do not try to hurry my Treasure. He is one that cannot be hurried. He must have time to sort his thoughts and he must feel the weight of a rider on his back before he moves a foot. You are no more to him than a fly, but let the warriors of Fionn sit astride of him from neck to tail, the tallest and the heaviest warriors. Then he will move."

Diarmid let himself down to the earth lightly, his fingers still knotted in the mane.

"Cunnaun," he said, "put your weighty limbs on this horse, and let the sixteen that come nearest to you in girth do the like by him. It may be that he will feel the bulk of a rider."

"Is it humour him? "cried Cunnaun. "If you bribed me with half the world, I would not put myself astride of that bare scraggy ill-jointed back-bone."

But warriors of the Fianna mounted till seventeen of them sat from head to tail. They took a tight grip with their knees. They drummed bountifully with their heels. The horse stood stock-still.

"You cantankerous splay-footed Image of Misfortune," cried Cunnaun, "does it task you to start without the weight of deep-chested Cunnaun? Stir yourself, you Drone!"

As he spoke he grasped the tail of the shaggy-coated horse and swung his weight upon it.

Deliberately the horse lifted hoof after hoof, and deliberately he set them down. He moved slowly at first as a swan moves when it leaves the water, balancing itself on its webbed feet. Then with a jolt, he quickened his pace till his riders rattled one against another like dried sticks in a high wind: and again he quickened his pace. Cunnaun thought it in time to loose his grip, but his hands refused: they clung to the tail of their own accord! And the horse quickened and quickened his pace, and the knees of the riders clung to him: and the riders were shaken, as barley is shaken on the winnowing floor, till there was no strength left in them. And Cunnaun swung at the tail till there was no strength left in him. When that horse came to a river, SPLASH! he was into it and over. When he came to a slanting hillside, B-R-R-R! he thundered down it. GALLUMPH! GALLUMPH! he went across the valleys. Trees raced past him; clouds raced past him; the sky itself raced past him, reeling: and behind him the warriors of Fionn raced, and Fionn himself raced, and all the hounds raced, panting and reeling as they ran.

At last a brightness appeared on the horizon, a level shining brightness, a brightness that moved glitteringly.

"The sea will stop them!" cried Fionn, and everyone drew a long breath and said to himself, "The sea will stop them!"

They could hear the thunder of its surf; they could see the widening depths of it; the runlets of foam at the edge. But the horse slackened speed not at all. SPLASH, he went through the wave-swirls; SPLASH, through the deepening water; SPLASH, SPLASH, through the glimmering wastes of the sea. SPLASH — SPLASH — SPLASH, till horse and man and riders slipped between sea and sky and went over the edge of the world.

Huddled on the empty sea-marge Fionn and his warriors looked at each other and at the giant hoof-tracks, part dry, part filling with brine. They had no words, and before their tongues were loosened again they were aware of two stranger youths moving towards them across the wet sands. Those youths were of one height and of one comeliness, and their coming was like the coming of sunlight in a thicket of green leaves: like the path of the wind in a field of silvery reeds. One held a whitely blossomed branch, the other had an axe of green stone socketed in the tooth of a sea-lion.

"We are come, O Fionn," they said, "to take service with you."

"Heed them not, Fionn," cried Cormac the Red, "one servant has snared you already, and these youths are, mayhap, from the elf-mounds: or they have come, mayhap, from beneath the sea-floor to entice us all to destruction."

"Nay," said Fionn, "but I will prove them first." And to the youths he said:

"What skill have ye, and what wisdom wherewith to serve?"

"I," said the axe-bearer, "can, with one blow and one turn of the hand, make a taut seafaring ship."

"And I," said the other, "can follow a trail over the sea and under the sea."

"Ye have come," said Fionn, "in a good hour. Make for me now a taut seafaring ship, and when I and those with me have embarked, urge her forward on the trail that is lost here in sea-spume."

The axe-bearing youth stooped and lifted a piece of driftwood from the beach; he struck the green stone axe upon it and flung it with one turn of his hand out on the waters. It lit there, as a seagull alights, and spread itself till it was a goodly seafaring ship. In the prow of it stood the lad with the silver branch.

"Aboard! "cried Fionn dashing into the surf.

"Aboard! Aboard!" shouted the Fianna, crowding into the sea, and soon they were swimming like otters and climbing over the sides of the ship. Steadily then, she moved forward: and through the dusk and through the hours of the night the lad in the prow followed the trail.

At dawn the ship came to rest under a cliff on the sheltered side of an island. The water there was coloured like an emerald, and the stone of the cliff was like silver: and like white silver it mirrored itself in the quiet waters. A path wound upwards dizzily, in loops and zigzags, and over the edge of the cliff leaned flowering shrubs and trees with branches green as jade, and in the branches bright-hued birds fluttered and called to each other.

"The trail touches land here," said the lad in the prow, "make fast the ship."

Diarmid was first to leap ashore. Bran, the hound came next. Soon Fionn and his warriors were climbing hand and foot, scrambling up the zigzags of the path. When they came to the top they found themselves in a forest of very ancient trees, and all the ground underfoot was starred with blossoms. On the twisted boughs of those ancient trees hung globed fruits, redder than pomegranates, and the air was heavy with their fragrance. Some of the warriors would have plucked them but the lad with the axe said:

"Do not reach a hand to these fruits; they are enchanted, and if you eat of one you will forget your father's home and your own country and your lovers there: and you will remain forever in this forgetful island."

And when they had walked for a great while in that forest and forborne the fruits, they came, all of a sudden, upon an open space of delicate close-growing grass. In the midst was a lake like the blue out-stretched wings of a butterfly, and in the sun-dazzle by the marge stood a youth. He had a cloak the colour of lapis lazuli, broidered with strange flowers and uncouth beasts. His hair was bound with a fillet of silver inset with ruby stones, and fell straight on either side of his face: it had a silvery brilliance as of falling waters.

"I greet you, stranger youth," said Fionn, "and would ask you for tidings."

"Ask naught of me," said the youth, "till a youth from your following, of one height and growth with myself, wrestles victory from me."

At this Diarmid the Brown-Haired stepped forth.

"I am of one height and of one growth with you," he said, "and may sun and wind and the deep-rooted earth give me the victory!"

They wrestled on the fine close-growing grass and it was a joy to the Flanna to look upon them: for in this wrestling there was swiftness as of hawks contending in mid-air; there was lithe alert sinewy grace and there was tough endurance. At times one, at times the other, had the upper hand in sturdiness and mastery. So, for long, and long, they contended. It was a cause of wonder to the Fianna that anyone should outmatch Diarmid, for he had been trained in wrestling by Angus Ogue – Angus the lovely laughing god who wanders the marts of the world and the by-ways, eternally young.

The shadows of the ancient trees lengthened on the fine grass, the lake made a little singing murmur. Diarmid, locked with his antagonist, bore heavily on him so that he tottered.

"The luck of Angus to you, Diarmid; the luck of Angus!" shouted the Fianna, and at the shout the stranger youth laughed and wound himself about Diarmid and leaped with him into the lake!

Wound together, they sank without commotion as a stone sinks. Diarmid's comrades, stock-still, watched the ripples widening on the empty waters.

"It is a grip of death and drowning," said Cormac the Red.

"Nay," said Fergus the Handsome, "Diarmid swims like a seal: he will come to the surface."

They watched for him – and the ripples widened slowly on the empty waters.

"A marvel," cried Fionn, "a marvel! The lake itself is sinking! Look! It is sinking into the earth!"

It was indeed sinking and sinking into cavernous depths; and leaving hollow mysterious spaces that deepened and deepened till the lake was far below them, glittering dimly.

Down they clambered through wan levels and from ledge to ledge; and as they climbed they had twilight about them and through the dusk they were aware of strange things – unicorns milky-white and white stags with branching horns of gold and trees with leaves of silver and crimson fruits.

And all the while the waters of the lake receded and receded. They gathered and globed themselves, moving with a soft radiance like a moon that had lost itself in this enchanted land and was burrowing a cave to hide in: and the Fianna climbed downwards through the dusk, and the moon that was a lake grew brighter, globing itself and glittering with frosted fire, till their eyes were dazzled by it, and suddenly Fionn cried out:

"This is no lake, glittering, but a palace: we have come now, of a surety, to the Land-Under-Wave – Mananuan's country!"

Each man looked then, with all the strength of his eyes, and saw the palace as it had been carved of one great crystal stone, rearing itself in towers and pinnacles: fantastic as a moon-bubble. Scarcely had their minds taken the wonder of it when they found themselves close upon the palace-threshold.

"A hundred thousand welcomes to Fionn, and the Fianna of Ireland," cried laughing voices, and all within there crowded a folk of such rainbow beauty that it seemed as if the light of the palace came wholly from them: they were like jewels or like stars.

"Greetings to you, Folk of the Gods of Dahna," said Fionn, "and greeting to him who is Silver Flame in the Land-Under-Wave. Fate, or good fortune, has brought me hither, seeking Diarmid the Brown-Haired."

Silver Flame, that was king there, came forward till he stood on the palace-threshold. Tall of stature was Silver Flame, and slender: and he outshone the others as Sirius, the Plumed Dancer, outshines the star-flocks.

"Fionn," he said, "Pulse of my Heart, you are welcome – and long expected! I have besought you many times, and my folk here have besought you, to come to the Land-Under-Wave."

"And I have refused," said Fionn, "because the green grass held my feet, and my hands had wherewithal to keep them busy on the ridge of the world."

"Yet through the ridge of the world we reached to you, and with every heart-throb, Fionn, you were aware of us: for every heart of man beats with the heart-beat of the earth; and some day, some night, some hour of the hours, must seek to us. But we, O Fionn, have sought to you, and in the day's work now you come to us. Enter, for Diarmid is here, and Cunnaun, and all who rode the shaggy tangle-coated horse."

When Fionn and the hunters and warriors with him crossed that threshold it seemed to them that after long wandering they had come home: it seemed as if night after night they had known the strangeness of this place in some impossible rapturous dream. Music of unearthly sweetness pulsed about them; it seemed as if they had heard it before the first word learned at a mother's knee.

And as they sat at feasting in this rich strangeness, Silver Flame leaned towards Fionn and said:

"Was not the bringing of you hither, Fionn, a thing well-done, in the lazy serving-man and the shaggy-coated horse?"

"It was well-done," said Fionn.

"Nay," said Cunnaun, "it was rough unkingly usage. Every son of misfortune who straddled and wriggled and rattled and sat askew – my grief! – on the pitiless edge of that knife-ridged back-bone while that Atrocity, that Tangled Mat of Ugliness, miscalled a horse, gambolled and frisked to his heart's content – every son of misfortune I say – has a grievance against you: and a double grievance have I, Cunnaun, who dangled shamefully at the tail. When he drove the loosened sods like flocks of birds into the air whom did they batter but myself? Whose countenance but mine was splashed with salt when he churned and trampled the sea-floor like behemoth and a crowd of dolphins and maddened sea-unicorns and whales?"

"Your words are edged with truth, Cunnaun," said Silver Flame, "I will make what amends you think fit."

"This, then, you shall do," said Cunnaun, "you shall bridle again that flat-footed, eye-offending, ramshackle quadruped and set seventeen of your warriors upon him; and find a personage of note and of importance, such as I am myself, to lay hold of his tail. Beside him the lazy servant shall run, and the horse shall splash across the sea, and spatter across the land till he comes to the green hill from whence he carried off myself and my comrades."

"It shall be so, Cunnaun," said the King of the Land-Under-Wave, Silver Flame, "and upon the white horses of Faeryland, Fionn, and Diarmid, and yourself, and the Fianna your comrades, shall journey back to that same hill."

When the feast had ended and they had drunken wine from Moy Mell, the Plain of Honey, and tasted fruits from the Land of Silver Fleece, the Folk of the Gods of Dahna led them forth by a door in a side of the palace away from that on which they had entered: they found themselves on a plain very thickly patterned with flowers.

"Bring forth now, for Cunnaun, the Earth-Shaker," said Silver Flame.

A crowd of youths led out a horse so dazzling white, so beautiful, that he was an astonishment to look on.

"This is a trick," cried Cunnaun, "for here is Mananaun's own horse!"

"Put an earth-shape on yourself!" said Silver Flame to the horse.

The horse stretched his proud neck and shook himself, and there he was for every eye to gaze on – the big, shambling, loose-jointed, tangle-coated, yellow horse! Seventeen of the joyous Folk of Dahna climbed on his back and sat there drumming mightily with their heels; another made himself bulky and bald-headed like Cunnaun and seized the tail.

"It is time to set out, my Jewel, my Treasure, my White Love," cried a loud laughing voice – and there was the big man! Every time he put a big flat foot down, the earth trembled: and every time the horse put a big flat foot down, the earth trembled a lot more.

"My blessing on you," cried Cunnaun, "and may your ride be as joyous as ours was!"

The horse neighed in answer, a high, screaming, ghostly neigh and all his riders burst into a roar of laughter, rattling on his high-pitched bare back-bone.

"It is farewell now for a little," said Silver Flame, "between the Folk of the Gods of Dahna and the warriors and hunters of Ireland: but ye shall not forget or lose the Land-Under-Wave. We shall be close to you when by the strength of your hands ye win victory, and closer to you in the hour of your defeat. Think on us, hunters of the Fianna, when your hounds bring down the forest boar: think on us when the antlered stag escapes you."

And while Silver Flame was speaking the plain was a-glimmer with white horses. The Folk of Dahna brought out for Fionn a noble stallion bridled with gold and with golden bells on the bridle-rein: and for each of the Fianna there was a white glimmering steed.

"It is farewell now," said Fionn, gathering up the reins, "to the Land-of-Heart's-Delight, for we must venture and endure on the ridge of the world. O Lords on whom the winds blow never roughly, we will sing you sagas of storm and hard battling and shipwreck when we come again. Farewell, a thousand times farewell!"

The youth who had wrestled with Diarmid stood close by Diarmid's horse, his hand upon the rein.

"Many a time you will come hither, Diarmid," he was saying, "for I have tied a knot of remembrance in the fringes of your mantle, and I will send a steed for you from Under-Wave if you will name your choice."

Then Diarmid bethought him of unicorns, golden-eyed, milky-white, that had slipped between the trees with silver leaves, and leaning over his horse's neck he whispered:

"Send a unicorn for me!"

THE SHINING BEAST

Once on a misty morning the thought came to Fionn that he would go hunting. He called the men of the Fianna and they took their hounds. The mist was so thick that the colour of one dog could scarce be seen from another, and the men of the Fianna wondered what this hunt would come to: but Fionn had the air of a man not to be questioned.

"My troth," said Cunnaun to Diarmid, "if we were waiting for venison till this hunt, we'd go hungry!"

"There's no knowing what we might find," said Diarmid, "on a morning like this."

"We might find a tree, or a cliff, or a mountain: with our heads," said Cunnaun, "for the matter of that! But it will task our wits to find our way home."

At this moment the mist lifted and they saw the Strange Beast. There was never a beast like it on the face of the earth. Its head was the head of a boar, save for the black twisted forest of horns on it. It had the bristling fell of a boar; and the body of a glancing stag; and feet like no animal under the sky: and strangest wonder of all, it had on either side of its body a shining moon. At once the Fianna loosed their hounds on it; and scarcely were they giving tongue in a good chorus, when the Red Woman came on them. Whatever wonder the beast was, the woman was greater. She was more than mortal-big in stature; her hair was redder than a carbuncle stone when the light shines through it, her garments were the colour of red embers; and her face had a glory of flame, like the sun in his rising.

"Clouds of misfortune and death!" said Cunnaun, "isn't it early in the day that destruction has found us! The Red Swineherd himself would be less to dread than this woman!"

"Call your hounds off the Beast that is out in front of them," cried the Woman, "for I, myself, am following it."

"For no woman and for no man born, will I call off my hounds," said Fionn, "it is my right to hunt on every hill and in every sheltered valley and wide-spread windy plain in Ireland. I am Fionn, chief of the Fianna."

"The Beast is mine," said the Woman, "and for thirty days and nights my feet have followed it; even since that hour when I started it by the Red Lake that is known to you as Lough Darrig. I must follow the Beast till he falls, if I would save the lives of my three sons. Therefore call off your hounds: for to no one but myself must the Beast fall."

"O Woman without sense," said Fionn, "you have no hounds, and mine are the best in the world. We will take the Beast and give it to you to work your will on."

"Loud-voiced and boasting are your words," said the Woman. "I myself am swifter than your hounds. I myself am stronger than the Fianna, and my right to hunt in Ireland is more ancient than yours."

Fionn laughed and cried, "Halloo!" to the hunting dogs, that all left him but Bran.

"I will follow the Beast, and cry hounds on it," he said, "and if there is might in you, stop me!"

At that the Woman changed herself to a great and terrible Serpent, a Wonder-Piast, towering up with every scale of her scales glittering like a ruby, glittering and changing with the redness of flame, and a mane of fiery spikelets rippling on her back like a forest of saplings. She twined herself about Fionn; she lifted him from the ground; she tightened her coils till his bones were like to have snapped; and she would have gotten the victory but for Bran that came out of the Faery Hills herself and had strength and power that belong to the Folk of Dahna. Bran made a great leap and took hold of the Piast by the throat: and as hard as the Red Piast squeezed Fionn, Bran squeezed the Red Piast.

"Call off your hound," cried the Red Piast.

"Loosen your grip of myself," said Fionn.

"Be it so," said the Red Piast, loosening her coils.

Bran took her teeth out of the Red Piast's throat. The Red Piast fell to the earth in a glittering heap. She gave herself one twist there, and changed her shape: she became a stream of running water, a tricklet of water, and sank into the earth. Fionn shook himself and his strength came back to him: and there was but Cunnaun and Diarmid and Lewy's Son with him, for the rest had followed the Beast and the hounds when he hallooed them on. And these three that were with him were as men rooted to the earth, nor could they move hand or foot or tongue till Fionn touched them.

"A blessing on your hand, Fionn," said Diarmid, "and let us follow the Beast, for there was never its like."

"It is a fool's chase," cried Cunnaun, "and we are part of the folly! Did not my heart foretell it?"

But Fionn hallooed Bran forward with a great "Halloo," and all three and himself followed her. It was drawing to evening when they came up with the other hounds and the rest of the men of the Fianna and the Strange Beast. And through the dusk and through the gloom that came after the dusk and through the hours of the night they followed the strange Beast. And always the two moons that were on either side of its body made a splendour about it, and always the swiftness of it was an astonishment; but with the waning of the night the moons began to abate in brightness and in the coldness of morning Fionn and his men were gaining on the Beast. Bran's jaws were snapping close to it, and the other hounds were hard upon Bran, when the Beast shook himself and shook out a great shower of blood upon the hounds and upon the men of the Fianna so that they were red from head to foot: but for all that they held to the hunt, and as the sun climbed into the sky they saw the Beast stagger to the Mountain of the King – that was called among the Fianna, Cnoc-na-righ – and when the Beast touched the mountain there came an opening at the foot of it and the Beast went in. When the Fianna reached the mountain the Red Woman was standing there. She had neither hurry nor concern on her.

"You did not take the Beast," she said, "your swift hounds did not outrun it."

"We did not, indeed," said Fionn, "but we know, and our hounds know, where the Beast is."

"I have that much knowledge myself," said the Woman, "and what is more, I have power to enter the hill. Have you courage to follow me, since you have followed so far?"

As she spoke, she struck the mountain with a druid rod and immediately a great door opened in the mountain and there came forth from it a sound of very sweet music.

"Courage is not wanting to us," said Fionn, "but we are stained and our garments are stained too redly; we would not show ourselves thus in a hill-palace."

She put a little horn that was carved from the bone of a sea-beast to her mouth, and blew a sharp shrill blast upon it. At the sound of the horn there came a huge brightly coloured bird from the mountain, singing and fluttering in the air and shaking gold dust from its wings. Following the bird came ten youths that were as beautiful as sunrise on snow-topped hills. They brought keeves of water for the cleansing of Fionn and his men, and garments for them that were as gay to look on as a blossomed field in summertime. When Fionn and the Fianna had clad themselves in this rich apparel the youths led them through the great door and into a vast hall that had the cool white radiance of the moon in it and the golden strength of the sun. The high vaulted roof was as it were carved from a single sapphire stone that had the blueness of the sky in it. The youths led them through the hall and into a nobler and more glorious chamber where sat a King like a great golden flower, so richly clad was he and so fair to look on. Musicians with viols and citharas and lutes, with harps and timpauns, with sweet-sounding flutes and bagpipes and chiming bells, made music for the King: and youths that were like bright-coloured birds danced and made music with their voices. The Red Woman stood by the King's chair. Her garments gave out a red light as though her body within them were flame, her countenance was too bright to look on, her hair that spread stiffly on either side of her face had the splendour of ruby stone.

"King of the Hill," she said, "this champion is Fionn, son of Moorna of the White Neck, of the Folk of Dahna. His hounds had strength to follow the Shining Beast for a day and a night, and he and the champions with him kept pace with the hounds: will you not of your generosity afford him a sight of the Shining Beast?"

"I will summon the Beast," said the King, "let the cup-bearers bring hydromel for the champions."

The cup-bearers of the King offered to Fionn and the Fianna hydromel from the land of the Ever-Young in goblets of crystal, and the Shining Beast came and stood before the King. The branching horns on his head had grown larger; the moons upon his body pulsed with light; his twisted spikelets of hair made forest patterns on the ridge of his back; his eyes glowed like two coals of fire. He made obeisance to the King.

"Shining One," said the King, "have no fear. I seek but to show you to these champions: from them and from the champions of the world you are safe, for I have put my protection upon you."

The Beast drew to his full height, and fire snorted from his nostrils. He stamped with his feet.

"Take back your protection," he cried, "that could not keep you from making a show of me! I put my faith in my own feet, I the swiftest runner in the world! I am going out in my own strength. I spurn the threshold of your door. I spit upon your protection and your power. Black clouds of misfortune upon you: and the sting of my words! You that can neither bind me, nor overtake me!"

Out from among them he went, like a flash. The Red Woman laughed and clapped her hands together.

"Your protection is broken, King of the Hill," she cried, "out, out – hound, and champion, and Folk of the Hill: follow the Beast!"

At her word they poured forth: the bright-coloured Folk of the Hill; the glorious King; the splendid radiant bird, fluttering and crying; the Fianna and their hounds; Fionn with Bran beside him. Far in front of them the Beast made a brightness, and after him they laboured, hound and man; for long they laboured vainly, but as the sun climbed higher and higher the shining of the Beast declined and his swiftness abated. There was blood marking his foot-tracks and he lurched heavily in his running. They gained on him little by little. Bran was the hound that came nearest him, but nearer still was the Red Woman, light and swift and radiant; a ruby shadow as it were of the Beast's brightness. When at last he fell it was she who stood beside him. It was in a wide treeless plain that the Beast crashed to the earth: he gave a great groaning cry and died. The sun was setting on the rim of the world and the Red Woman standing there was redder than the sun.

When Fionn and the Fianna and the hounds and the Folk of the Hill came up, they did not see the Shining Beast. They saw a man that had the strength of an oak tree lying dead. His outlandish garments were stiff with gold all thickly wrought to images of birds and serpents and flying dragons. His hair was twisted in a ring of malachite: a bush of hair it was, branching in spikelets and curls and knots; and every knot and curl and spikelet was of a different colour and had a jewel flaunting and shining in it. One side of his face was white as a bleached bone, the other side was ebon black.

"Keep out from him," cried the Red Woman, "there is venom of the adder in every thread of his garments, and venom in *every* spikelet of his hair, and in every jewel that he is pranked with!"

The sun flung a last redness on the world and sank, but the dead man there in his lavish adornment shone with a smouldering splendour as if his robes and jewels had fire in themselves. Lying there he made an eye-offending evil omened brightness.

The Red Woman stooped and lifted a handful of earth: she let some of it fall through her fingers on the forehead of the dead man.

"Since this King is dead," she cried in a high chanting voice, *"my son that is a Poet can make songs again."*

She let some of the earth fall on the dead man's breast.

"Since this King is dead, my son that is a Master of Wisdom will have peace for meditation."

She let some of the earth fall on the dead man's feet.

"Since this King is dead, my son that carves in stone and ivory can make images again, of men and beasts and flying dragons – at his will."

She threw the rest of the earth lightly on the dead man from head to foot.

"You that had the swiftness of the wind," she said, *"and the untameable heart of the wind – go with the wind!"*

At her word the body of the dead King that had been the Shining Beast began to shrivel and shrivel and change till it was nothing but a brightly coloured leaf, and the wind blew it away. The Red Woman turned herself to Fionn:

"You had a share in this King's death," she said, "and it may be that ill-fortune will fall upon you. For myself there is neither good nor evil fortune more. I go to the Land of the Ever-Shining Ones: and I will take you, and these the Fianna with you, and your hounds into that country where but to wish is to have your asking."

"I would not leave Ireland – the hills and valleys of it," said Fionn, "if your offer were seven times as good. If there is one with me who would go, let him go."

"We also choose Ireland," cried the Fianna.

But Cunnaun grumbled, "It is too many boastful words we have, and our stomachs empty. Had I not truth on my tongue when I said this hunt would be without venison?"

"It shall not be without venison, Bald Cunnaun," said the Red Woman, "yonder is a stag!" And indeed at that moment a great red stag bounded past them, careless of the dogs: and joyously all those hounds cried on his track! Gladly the Fianna followed them in the cool twilight and the hunt went towards the Glen of the Thrush, that is called Glen-na-Smole: but when they were come to the dewy river-margin of that glen the stag was still before them, bounding easily, careless of the dogs, and not even Bran had gained the breadth of a pig's snout upon him. A young sickle moon was growing brighter in the sky and shadows were thickening in the glen.

"We will call off the hounds," said Fionn, "it is not wise to trust this valley in the moonlight."

"Well said! My Heart," exclaimed a laughing voice beside him – and there was the Red Woman again!

"Oh call the hounds off," said Cunnaun, "we were fools that cried them on. There is no venison in this hunt."

"There is venison, Bald Prophet," said the Red Woman, and from her mantle she took a small slender hound that was as white as snow on a mountain top. The eyes of that hound were as blue as gentian blossom, and his ears were as red as the buds on an apple tree growing wild in an alder-thicket. The Red Woman cried him on the stag, and with a turn of his head and a twist of his body he brought it down and left it lifeless on the ground. "That is for you, Cunnaun," said the Red Woman, and lifting the hound in her mantle she went laughing away.

"Fionn," said Cunnaun, "it's many a time I gave you good advice though the wisdom of it was bitter, and now I will give you a good advice. Do not meddle with that stag lest we never have done with enchantments. It is in my thought that when we turn our backs upon him he will get to his feet and move away, easy and careless. It is not at this hour of the night I would care to find myself in the Land-Under-Wave, or maybe in Balor's Country itself. It is not listening to the screaming of witches and headless demons I would be this night – the way you were when you went into the enchanted hut in the valley of the Ancient Yew Tree! Let us turn our steps towards Aloon where there is mead and ale for a multitude. Wild fowl of the marshes will not be wanting to us, nor wild boars roasted with honey and apples, nor the flesh of bulls. Singers will sing to us and candles will be lit."

"Yes," cried Diarmid, "let us go, Fionn. We have a tale to tell to-night."

"What word has Bran on it?" asked Fionn.

Bran rubbed her muzzle into his hand and started for Aloon.

THE NUTS OF KNOWLEDGE

Fionn, the son of Uail, the son of Bassna, the son of Trenmor, sat by the Tarn of the Shadow within a stone's throw of the Sacred Mountain of Slievenamon. It was Sowan Eve, chill and silent. One or two venturesome stars looked through the dusk. The plain was empty. Fionn's thoughts did not stray there as they might have strayed among things well remembered: his mind was not occupied with the stars. His mind centred itself upon the Tarn of the Shadow: for there, upon the dark waters – at some hour, some one moment of the night – the Shadow of Sive the Goddess would glimmer like flame.

To-night Sive the Goddess would descend from Slievenamon: unseen, she would descend; by unknown pathways. Unseen, she would cross the plain; she would cross the green ridge of the world; and at the world-edge she would lift the curtains of the sky and drop them silently behind her; for, to-night, she would visit the Well of Knowledge, the Well of the Hazel Trees, in the Country of the Ever Young.

To-night, the Well of Wisdom, the Fountain of Youth, would be stirred by the gorgeous fins of the Salmon of Knowledge: mightily, to-night, the Salmon would winnow with his fins, and the Well would rise in surges of crimson and purple – in nine waves of crimson and purple – and overflow in five streams, nourishing the stars and the lives of men. Sive would draw water from the Well. She would turn again and pass this way, Fionn knew, to Slievenamon; unseen, and yet her shadow – a flickering brightness – would fall on the tarn close to him; and if in that moment he cried out her Name – she would stay her steps – she would give him a draught of the Water. When it wetted his lips he would know the secrets of the earth and of the places under the earth. He would know what the birds of the air said to each other, and what the beasts said – knowledge befitting a champion and the chief of a great clan.

If only he could watch unblinking till the sun climbed the horizon. Nine days he had fasted in preparation: he wished now that he had fasted longer – hunger prods a man to wakefulness. He wished that he had a comrade by him to change words with, but that did not come into the adventure. He thought of the Well of Knowledge. To-night the Scarlet Hazel Trees that leant above it would drop their fruits upon its waters, and the ripples they stirred in falling, purple and scarlet, would spread and twinkle and vanish where those five streams issued that refreshed the world; and wakened there and rising from the depths, Fintan the

Salmon of Knowledge would show himself, jewelled and glittering, scale on scale. Sive would look into the depth of the Well. She would see the faces of Gods – proud imperturbable faces – down: far down; and tangled stars; and black unfathomable night. She would dip a golden pitcher and draw a draught of the well-water – sweet and bitter – she would lift it shoulder-high and turn her steps again to Slievenamon. Tonight she would pour a wisdom-draught for the Gods of Dahna – the Folk of the Gods of Dahna whom age cannot wither.

The subtly-smiling beautiful Folk of Dahna, the Riders upon White Horses: '*Upon their heads they have close curling golden hair: their eyes are blue like ice: good they are at man-slaying.*'

He, Fionn, was kin to them: he had feasted with them: nay more – had wrestled and fought with them. What a night it was when he slew Allyn, son of Midna, and won back the lordships that his father had: while earth and heaven flamed together. What a day it was when they crowded round him: the warriors, young and eager, shouting his name; the champions, sword hardened lauding him – Fionn the Warrior, Fionn the Ruler of Clann Morna!

What a game it was – the sword game. A man never wearied of it: and in the end it brought him death with the war-shout in his ears, and afterwards the keening of a warrior and proud burial. Age cannot wither the sword! It is an ugly, limping, malefic, toothless thing – old age! There is no one who would not wish to be ignorant of it – as ignorant as the Folk of the Gods, whose fingers cannot stiffen on the sword-hilt.

It was Sowan-Tide – the Night of the Laughter of the Gods – to-night. Their palaces flamed to-night upon the heights and windy ridges of the world; and across the far-stretching plains – wide open. To-night a mortal could enter there: could drink, ungrudged – from vats of mead and hydromel – the golden-beaded heady drink of immortals.

A pulse leaped in Fionn's heart at the thought – and out of nowhere a wind swept down the empty spaces of the night. It beat upon the earth thunderously, it rent the fleeces of the sky, and through it Fionn heard the faint sweet silvery music and the singing voices of the Faery Folk:

Forget the hearth,
    Forget the roof,
Set the wheel aside:
Leave your weaving,
    Warp and woof,
Steal out to us this Sowan-Tide.

Steal out to us, our tossing hair
Sets suit and moon and stars aflare.
The racing winds are hounds beside
The cloud-maned horses that we ride.

Come ride with us, have heart to dare
The plunging steed; the steeps of air;
The swirling, high, tumultuous flight,
The aery hooves – this Sowan-Night!

The Faery Host – plumed with every colour of beauty – the Horsemen of the Sky, were passing; they were calling to him.

"Go your ways, Proud Lords of the Air," cried Fionn, "lighter than wind on your bright-necked horses. If ye are wise ye will envy me to-night!"

He struck his hands together for warmth, and kept his eyes steadfastly on the tarn. In some place far away rose the ullaloo of a wolf. A wolf answered it. The night grew colder. Slowly the wheel of the stars, turning, measured the hours. Fionn could but guess how it turned, for he dared not lift his eyes from the tarn lest he should miss that moment, that smallest moment, when the shadow of Sive would burn and flicker there – the shadow of the unseen Goddess that was Flame – it was not in his power to consult the wheeling stars. Slowly the hours passed. Fionn dipped his fingers between the reeds and touched them to his forehead – at that moment the water kindled!

"SADB," he cried.

The silvery flame was stayed among the reeds of the tarn.

Upon the thither side of the water she stood. Her beauty was terrible. Her beauty was like a sword that twisted in his heart. Her beauty like a flame destroyed him. There was no strength left in him: the marrow was dried in his bones.

And she stood there with the Universe behind her, with the Crowned Gods of Dahna rank on rank – and he could not raise his head: could not raise an eyelid.

"What is your will?" she said.

It was a voice so faint and sweet and small that it seemed to be within Fionn himself that it spoke.

Fionn knew that every mountain in Ireland stood alert for his answer.

He would fain have cried:

"To see you, to see *You* – only once – only once!" but his tongue refused him, and the sword of her beauty twisted deeper and deeper in his heart. He moaned like a hurt beast. He flung out his arms convulsively and fell forward with his face on the earth.

His body sagged limply.

How light, how unburdened it felt to be dead. He had not thought that he could feel so light. What a greenness, as of emerald-stone, about him: a strange translucent greenness that caressed his body – endless, unobstructed, softly-sliding, translucent greenness. He moved without effort, sustained and poised in it. It lapped him intimately, it yielded to every wish. The empty spaces of this world were his: no moon chilled them, no fierceness of the sun burned there, no sprinkled stars. And like the pellucid vastness in which he moved, his body was vast: and in a measure strange to him. The strangeness pleased him, a sense of the mysterious deeps below him filled him with joy. He joyed in himself. He floated in his world; he cleft it with swift strokes; he swam strongly in it. It was a world of waters – swirling, emerald-pale, iridescent. How the ripples of it played against him as he swam: how the bubbles of it danced and blossomed in foam. What a pulse, what a long slow surge of delight went through it, lifting him, intoxicating him. He was swimming in the Well of the Sacred Hazels. He was the crimson-spotted Salmon of Knowledge!

And the Nuts of the Sacred Hazel Tree fell on the Waters.

They were like strange fruits, golden-rinded, ruby-hearted, fragrant, wonderful: and as they fell the circling water crimsoned, a surge of ecstasy moved in it, and everywhere a myriad joyous voices cried:

"Exult!
Exult!
The stars blossom.
Wisdom is born.
Exult!"

Fionn that was the God of the Waters, exulted. Beauty flowered in him; Wisdom unfolded. With every surge, with every pulse, with every heart-beat, Fionn exulted.

And still the fruits of the Hazel Tree fell upon the waters.

Like stars they fell, like glittering constellations, like flaming suns. And still the voices cried:

"Exult!
Exult!
Exult!"

But with Fionn it was different. The splendour overwhelmed him; the ecstasy beat him down: as heavy rain beats down the flowering branch, as the torrent overwhelms the swimmer. Those voices that had cried out the very cry of his heart were alien now. He must escape from them or die. If he could hide in the depths, if he could find a shelter in the darkness, if he could be a waterweed in the cleft of a rock, forgotten, he might live – Fionn who knew so much, who had dared so much.

He had but a moment in which to choose. Wide-eyed he made the choice. Gathering all his strength he thrust his splendid body upwards in the salmon-leap. Into the flaming ether, into the intolerable ecstasy, he shot with winnowing fins and thrashing tail: a thousand colours flashed and faded on his scales: he whirled – a splendour – in that splendour of suns!

"Exult!" he cried, as he somersaulted, *"Exult! EXULT!"*

The radiance wounded him at every pore. He gasped and choked in the death-agony. He slid endlessly through space, fathom after fathom, league upon league, till the Abyss engulfed him.

The sun had not yet climbed the horizon. The world was silver-pale. There was a light frost on the grasses, a light snow had feathered the summit of Slievenamon: everywhere there was stillness and cold. Fionn stirred uneasily: he clenched and unclenched a hand. He raised his head: he gathered himself together and sat up. The Tarn of the Shadow was like a mirror of polished findruiney. The motionless ash tree beside it was jewelled with crystal in every branch; naked it stood against the violet sky: low down a solitary star burned faintly like a forgotten torch.

Fionn rubbed the calves of his legs.

"Goll would laugh at the sight of me," he said, "Fionn that cozened himself with a dream – like a starved bodach!"

"Ha! ha! ha!" laughed a bird in the ash tree. "Morning-wisdom like the headache after a feast!"

"What thing are you?" asked Fionn.

"I am an Image of the Sun," cried the bird, spreading arrogantly the great wings of a ger-falcon.

Fionn leaped to his feet: strength filled him: life danced and sang in him: his heart beat with the mighty pulsations of the earth: he felt the surge of the Sacred Well: he remembered the terrible beauty of Sive: he heard the stones whispering: he heard the small sharp song of the frost: and he heard the shout of the sun, advancing like an army with banners.

"What am I – what then am I?" he said, half to himself.

"Ha! ha! ha!" laughed the frosted grasses. "Here comes one who has drunken of the Well of Knowledge. What are we? What are the patterned stars? What is the sun? Ask a new riddle – for once!"

EDITOR'S NOTE

In the copy of The Tangle Coated Horse *on which we drew to edit this collection, on the inside of the back page, Ella Young had written out her poem "Vale", signed it and dated it "April 19, 1956" – only 3 months before her death. The book was inscribed to her friend, Margaret Lyall, in the following words:*

"Be laughter with you, laughter of sun and wind and running stream; and song of thrush and ousel and high-soaring lark!"

We decided to include the poem here, though it originally appeared in Seed of the Pomegranate, and other poems *and then again in* Smoke of Myrrh, and other poems. *Clearly it was a very important poem to Ella Young, and she felt that it should be placed here. We can only agree that it makes a deeply moving footnote to her work and a fitting conclusion to the first part of this collection.*

VALE

Should I not, at the ending of my days,
Praise Life and Love and Death? Praise Love that sings
First song and last, triumphant Love that flings
A net about the stars, strong Love that stays
Time's hound in leash, and threads the labyrinth maze
Of hopes and fears unsnared, spreading great wings
Against disaster: Love, proud Lord, that brings
The world to nothingness. Yea, Love, I praise.

Praise fleeting joys and hours once treasure-store,
Praise sweetness of the viol and the flute,
Rather buds that died and dawns that flame no more,
(Ephemeral blossoms of a bitter root)
Praise Life, the dancer in a motley suit,
And last praise death, bursting the prison door.

PART TWO:

AUTOBIOGRAPHY AND UNPUBLISHED WRITINGS

Ella Young with close friend artist John O'Shea. Monterey Peninsula, California. No date.

EXTRACTS FROM
FLOWERING DUSK
(1945)

Ella Young's autobiography Flowering Dusk[1] *is a curious and often moving document which deserves to be better known. All who wish to understand the remarkable woman who wrote the stories and poems we have edited here should read it. We can only give extracts here, but encourage readers to seek out copies of this rare title.*

The first extract reveals Ella's "methodology." For twenty-five years she lived with locals in many remote areas of Ireland and gathered the stories and faerytales which she later turned into prose and poetry. She learned the old language and the old ways of an Ireland on the brink of great change. In 1925 when the treaty with England forced a division of her beloved country, Ella came to America. In the second extract we see that she brought with her the spirit of adventure and magic that defined her life in Ireland.

1: ANOTHER GLIMPSE OF THE WEST

It is almost dusk, and I am walking along a road that is strange to me. Someone should have met me at the little railway station with a jaunting car. Nobody did. I am bound for a farmhouse. Some kind folk have pointed out the road. I must walk. There is a strange delight in following an unknown road at dusk. It lengthens out, it takes strange shapes; some adventure lies at the end of it, one seems to think. I had no idea how far off the house was or how long it would take me to get there. The magic of the West held me, as it always did. It didn't seem to matter whether I found a house.

Why had no one come to meet me at the railway station? I had taken such trouble to find out from a railway guide exactly when that train would arrive at Cong. (And this, of course, was silly, since everyone in the West knew exactly when a train arrived, an event like a thunderstorm

---

1   *Reproduced courtesy of Random House*

or a meteor.) Why hadn't they come? This question was beginning to eat into my mind, beginning to spoil the mystery of the unknown road, and the twilight with song of thrush and blackbird in it. The emptiness of the road, the darkening sky, gave me a sense of going on and on, over the edge of the world. But a clatter of horse hooves and wheels asserted itself and round a corner an Irish jaunting car came into sight. The man who drove was standing on the dashboard to drive more effectively. He drew up with a flourish.

"Are you the lady from Dublin?"

"Yes, I am," I said in an injured tone. "Why did no one meet the train? Did you get my letter?"

"We got no letter. We thought you were not coming. But a while ago my mother said, 'Take the car and go out to meet her. She is on the road.'"

"What could have happened to the letter?" I asked, safely ensconced in the car. "Oh, it's the postmistress," said he. "She keeps the hotel in the town and opens all the letters from tourists. If no one meets them at the train she is there to talk about the hotel." That made me suddenly remember that someone had spoken to me of the hotel and suggested that I spend the night there. But I was determined to be far from the sound of a railway train.

A warm welcome awaited me in the small farmhouse. The woman of the house, dignified and pleasant-faced, came out to help me from the car. The daughter, a shy young girl with red-gold hair, was there too. In the background stood the father of the family. My driver was the red-haired, only son. Firelight and tallow candles made a brightness in the house.

My bedroom smelt heavily of peat smoke. (I learned afterwards that in some occult fashion that room gathered to itself any smoke that might be going loose about the house.) But dominating the peat smoke, dominating the room, was a sense of the country outside, passionately alive, rejoicing in itself – strong, strong and beautiful in the darkness. I could hardly wait for dawn light to see it.

A country of stone, with colours no grassland can take: purples that lightened to amethyst, pale reaches of silver, blue that rivalled lapis lazuli, faint fugitive touches of rose. The lakes it had did not give greenness. Their waters were still and black. What did that country remember? Something too old for man. He had no part in the fantasy of its rocks, in the dark steely glitter of its waters. Hawks could live there. Hawks and the Gods of Dana. Like jewels, like the colours of dawn and sunset, like unearthly flowers, the Gods of Dana moved in the desert of stone, showed themselves in the haunted knolls. White horses, a flaunt of many-coloured mantles, strange headdresses they had. Like a hound before them and following them went the wind. Music swirled and sounded about them. It was good for a man to veil his eyes as they passed. They were out of the old, old life of the earth – before the glaciers had ribbed these rocks and scooped these hollows – they would be there when ice again gave quietness to the world.

The country-folk had stories of giants and dwarfs, of kings whose burial mounds made the only hills in the landscape. A great battle between gods and demons had raged once from horizon to horizon.

"Do you see yon tall standing stone?" said the son of the house as the jaunting car rattled past it. "A great king lies under it. His name was Lugh Lamh-fada."

How well I knew that name! Lugh the Long-handed, the Sun God, Lugh Ildana, the Master of every Craft, the Champion of the Gods – Lugh, under that stone, dead! But his great white Hound still coursed the heavens, and dying folk yet prayed for dawn.

By the turf fire in the stone-flagged kitchen we sat, night after night, talking: the household and myself. Candlelight made slight inroad on the darkness, but the turfs were warmly red. We talked of prophesies; of saints that had the power to bless or curse; of golden cups and buried treasure; of boats that sped over lonely inhospitable waters where the living dared not venture; of folk who made fortunes in America, the New Island, as they called it – feeling it closer by them than Dublin town, nearer than Tara, once so spend-thrift of wine and song – Tara, where their ancestors had foregathered with kings.

At last I had to go. The horse was in the shafts of the jaunting-car, my meagre travelling kit hoisted across the threshold, and the household gathered in the open air to bid me farewell: the man of the house, the golden-haired daughter, the son who had handled the reins on so many journeys across bog and stone-land, and the woman of the house. In Gaelic Ireland the woman is always the head of the house. This woman, gracious, kindly featured, nimble-witted, had been most kind to me. I thought of her as I thought of the country itself, with joy and respect. She came forward now to speak for the group. She said: "You will go far away from here, and with time you will forget this place and us, but we will never forget that a great saint once stayed in our house."

She kissed my hand. I could not find any words.

"A Great Saint!"

Would I in the long years of a lifetime forget that! I never dared to publish it. I never dared make trial of it on my family. But one reason why I write these memoirs is that I may record it here.

2: THE RATTLESNAKE

Deirdre and I are riding through the woods on Lobo Mountain. The trees in this part are fairly tall, and the trail is fairly easy. We are riding carelessly when suddenly my eye is caught by a very beautiful pine tree, tall, red-stemmed and straight. It stands a little apart from its fellows. Something at the root of it moves, a gorgeous something, green and gold, freaked and freckled with patterns.

"A gorgeous snake. What luck," I cry to Deirdre, who is riding several paces behind me. Next moment I take note of the flat triangular head, and shout to Deirdre, "Go back, it's a rattlesnake!"

We wheel our horses about and are riding slowly away, when suddenly a thought occurs to me. That rattlesnake, so big, so splendid? Ever since I came to America I had longed to see a rattlesnake coiled and hissing. I had asked the Nature Powers to let me see one. I had explained to them that I wanted to see the rattlesnake when no person would kill it: I wanted to see it with someone who thought snakes were strange splendid things. I had waited for years for this gift from the Nature Gods. Here it was now, and I was riding away from it! I pulled up my horse at once.

"Deirdre," I said, "we are fools to leave that rattlesnake."

"But the horses won't go back," said Deirdre, "they won't stand. Your horse, Prince, will go wild when he sees it's a rattlesnake."

"No, he won't!" said I. "Prince is my good friend. I'm going to explain it all to him and ask him to go back."

A split second explained it to Prince – that is the good of being pals with a horse! He promised to go back and stand. When we went back, the rattlesnake was coiled and hissing. He had taken two twists and the rest of his body stood up. His head was bent forward and swayed from side to side. His tongue flickered, and his rattle, which had eight or nine rings, vibrated sharply. The sun struck the red bark of the tree and touched up the vibrant green and gold of the rattlesnake.

A snake, I had been told, can strike only his own length. I made a rough calculation of his length and halted Prince just outside of striking distance – Deirdre came to a stop on the mare, Bobchuile, much farther off. Prince stood without moving an eyelash.

The solitude of mountain-peak on mountain-peak was about us. The desert was stretched below, a multicoloured sea. The world held just ourselves, the horses, and the snake.

I think the snake knew that we were not deadly enemies.

He continued to sway, and he increased the vibration of his rattle, but he made no attempt to strike. He was marvellous to look at. When I had filled my eyes and my imagination with that sinuous splendour, I said to Prince:

"Turn quietly and go quietly away."

He went quietly away.

"Wasn't it splendid?" Deirdre and I chorused to each other.

"That green snake," said Deirdre, "is a very rare kind. If anyone knows that it is here they will come up and hunt it for its skin."

"We must swear an oath never to tell," said I.

"Good idea," said Deirdre.

We swore the oath.

3: EVALUATION

The days and years of my life, fair-faced or evil-countenanced, the good gifts, the bitter honey, the mandragore, the forgotten and unforgotten, what do they mean?

Black teeth on white, and a child to wonder at them!

At end of all, what does one have when one is old? Some wisdom – perhaps; many memories, certainly; and if one is lucky, a feather shaken from the Phoenix-Bird.

I walked in the Land of the Ever-Living with my Ladye. We walked in a wood. It was a wood that had the naked loveliness of Springtime, and yet the boughs were glad with blossoms. A wind moved with us, and where it touched the delicate grass under foot slender-stemmed hyacinths sprang up. There was music everywhere and changing colour and motion. The trees changed shape and stood a-tiptoe for very lightness of heart.

I have said that we walked in the wood: equally the wood walked in us. It moved with us, the trees blossomed in us. The music, the wind, the flowers in the grass patterned our mood; and we patterned the trees: growing tall with their tallness, reaching out joyously with their branches. The music that surged and sounded everywhere was like the heartbeat of our blood.

It would seem as I tell this, that I was thinking more of the wood than of my Ladye, but I was thinking more of my Ladye: for walking beside her again I was whole. I had no wish unfulfilled.

FAERIE MUSIC

(CEOL SIDHE)

Extracts from Ella Young's unpublished diary for 1917-1918 with later notes made in 1952. Ella wrote hastily in her diary with little concern for punctuation. We have added this only as necessary for clarity.[2]

Many people in Ireland hear the Faerie Music. Sometimes it is a tune that can be written down and set to words, or a reel that can be played on the bagpipes, but when described by people who have heard it over a length of time it is described as orchestral. AE, poet and mystic, heard this music over a period of years and described it as orchestral. His wife, the beautiful Violet North, told me when I spoke of Wagnerian music that she did not care to listen to Operas and Symphonies because the Faerie Music was so much beyond anything that mortal instruments could produce... More than once it happened that I was on a hillside with people who heard this music and drew my attention to it, but I was conscious only of the mingled sounds that anyone could hear on an Irish hillside.

Suddenly, and unrepentantly, the power was given me in Achill. The music as I first heard it was orchestral and of amazing richness and complexity.

Since that Achill morning I have heard the music many times, in many places both in Ireland and in America where the composer, Henry Cowell, whose music has stirred so much controversy and interest, spoke to me of Faerie Music that he heard on the Dunes at Oceano, and at other places where he could wander solitary.

I believe that many people will be aware of this music, as one by one they draw closer to Nature, and have quietude and a heart that waits to listen. I had an opportunity to listen under very favourable circumstances, and kept an account of what I heard.

---

2 *Source: Huntington Library*

These leaves from a diary contain notes on Faerie Music as I heard it on the side of Maulin Mountain in County Wicklow, Ireland, during a period lasting from August the 20th 1917 to February 12th 1918. E.Y.

1917

Sunday 26th [August]: During the afternoon of the day I heard the music of a reel played very quickly. The music (i.e. tune) changes two or three times but the reel continues for a long while. Not much sound after sundown but after ten o'clock I heard a music as of innumerable cymbals. This changed from multitudinous sound of silver bells and again to great bells tolled slowly. There finally played a little wistful tune.

Monday 27th: Rained in a steady downpour all day and as far as I know through the night … I woke to hear wonderful music … It came on with a certain monotony, like slow-moving waves. On the crest of each wave there was a running melody, and as spray curling on a wave-top takes one's eye this caught one's ear … with the exception of the music in the Curraun Achill this was the most wonderful and beautiful music of the Sidhe that I have ever heard. I woke later in the night out of a dream because I heard the loud sound of voices outside. Voices as if two people calling out questions and replies to each other as they walked … the men passed close under my window, one of them singing a snatch of an air in a high lilting voice. It was only when I wakened more fully that I knew they could not be mortals … the voices had the peculiar quality of voices one hears in the wind or by streams.

Tuesday 28th: At night a great burst of music … then a curious melody obtruded itself in which there was a dominate high note as high as the highest note on a piano but with a tone the volume such as no instrument that I know could produce. I heard also a music as of stricken anvils: as if a myriad smiths hammered out a music … I heard, as it were, a great litany with chants and responses and at times I caught the words, but they were in a language I don't understand. Several times I heard the words Abaktha … myetho and the word Wyehoo was repeated monotonously in a chant: wyehoo, wyehoo, wyehoo, wyehoo, wyehoo.

Wed, 29th: Showers and wind. In the afternoon I heard a great trumpet blown on the mountain Maulin and a burst of trumpets following the first. At night, music of bells. cymbals, harps, violins and instruments that I cannot liken to anything.

30th Aug: At darkfall I heard only one instrument like a glorified Jew's harp. On this a tune was played over and over again and through it came the sound of a high, clear voice singing. The wind rose later and I heard the sound of men's voices singing in the wind; when I listened to them I became aware of many voices chanting as if it were a litany with responses and long chanted Gregorian rhythms. All the other music seemed hushed, but I think it was going on all the time … the voices excite and weary me. I woke before dawn and heard the most wonderful music: delicate, intricate rhythms with the most exquisite melodies interwoven … a myriad, myriad instruments produced this music. I was able, in it, to approach Djouce Mountain – the music became Djouce as if the very Heart of Peace became music and this is not music that I can describe – it is beyond words.

31st Aug: At Darkfall heard a melody with a strong marked third beat which was emphasized by an instrument like a muffled drum. What instrument produced the melody I do not know. If drops of water could be made to produce sounds, as harp strings do, they might give such notes.

1st Sept: Melodies on harp strings all day … the wind came in a gust with the sound of a great clanging in it – small silvery bells sounding everywhere … Heard a melody which I had heard several times the other night but was much disturbed by a voice in the wind crying "Beeya, Beeya, Beeya, Beeya, Beeya, Beeya, Beeya." Woke later in night and heard a great horn march of the wind which was sweeping down from Lough Bray. An orchestra with a great number of wind instruments, helped by an organ, could have reproduced the music in a coarse fashion. There were innumerable small drums and cymbals and pipes with great drums and strong trumpets and instruments of loud sounding bass and a curious reedy instrument the like of which we have not.

3rd Sept: I understood the tales of people on hillsides who have heard a faery music and are compelled to dance till they drop exhausted. They have, perhaps, done nothing more than listen as I did (part of the time against my will) and imagine that they have danced.

8th Sept: My head has been for several days quite normal and I have heard only the ordinary sounds. This morning early, I heard a number of voices singing in unison with strange instruments. Most were rhythms that I had not heard before but I did not allow myself to listen. I think that by listening too intently I had strained my astral sense of hearing. I think the singing in my head was really astral.

4th Oct: Last night at darkfall I heard the most wonderful music … I had been aware of a wandering music all day. This music came suddenly – a wonderful orchestral effect. A burst of sound in great trumpets as if the riders of the Sidhe advanced rank after rank on mighty horses. Against this music came a sudden wave or gush like a swirl of wind but really full of all sounds of music. It broke against the trumpet's sound like starry fire and overwhelmed it for a little.

9th Oct: I have been hearing music all these days and voices crying … Last night about 8:30 Irish Sun time the wind rose suddenly as it does here. There was a sound of trumpets – and very sweet percussion instruments accompanied by a sound which I could not liken to anything. As the sound came nearer I knew that it was of a multitude of voices singing. After a little the trumpet sound stopped but the percussion instruments continued as long as I listened. The wind swept up in gusts and each gust was full of these voices – myriads – a confused clamour at times, yet with a rhythm: a high sweet sound and deep low Gregorian effects. At times I could almost distinguish the words. They seem to consist of separate phrases chanted or sung; several of them at the same time by different groups. If to some ear somewhere the confused broken sounds of a large city made intricate music it might resemble the music of these voices. The voices have not the solidity of human voices, they are high reedy whispering voices and seem to be in the wind … one clear mocking voice cried with the greatest distinctions Balaclóo, Balaclóo. That same word was chanted by many voices also Beeya etc.

12 Oct: This morning I heard a voice singing a long slow rhythm that seemed to have the sadness…of all the world in it. The voice was rich and sweet – held on long sustained notes. It had not the super human beauty of the Voice which is Djouce [Mountain] but it was very strong and beautiful…

17th Oct: Last night I was aware of Gregorian chants and many voices singing. The sound increased in volume and the rhythm became very intricate … most lovely filling me with a sense of freedom and exultation. The voices chanted words or phrases … Hy Bermillu, Hy Dramel, Heroó, Wyehóobilik and Kyeyóubilik, Wyehóo, Balalóo etc. These were chants of different groups … no description can do justice to this music: the intricacies … the changing rhythms. The way in which a sound is echoed and re-echoed … Yet I am convinced that in the material world these sounds would merely be different sounds produced by the wind in trees – in the astral they sound as I have described. In the domain of Powerscourt [an estate near Bahana] are very beautiful silver-frosted pines and cypresses and monkey-puzzle trees as well as beech, larch and Scotch fir. These trees and the wind make the singing. I am now able to listen for a long time without getting tired and I hear all the sounds without having to listen intently as at first. The sounds are loud.

18th Oct: A Giant Voice came up the valley shouting some phrase that I could not distinguish – a deep very loud voice – so loud that it seemed impossible that the whole neighbourhood for miles round did not hear it as well as myself. Later, I hear very loud music of bells accompanied by some unknown instrument: and later music of bagpipes … I notice one great difference between this music and the music in the material world: it is difficult to recall the music and the sensation it produced. Beautiful music heard in the material world I can recall most vividly and live again through the sensations it produces. The astral music is very much in sound delicately beautiful – to hear it gives me extraordinary pleasure but in trying to recollect it, it seems bodiless, unsubstantial.

1918

12th Feb: At half past nine (Sun time) I heard a bell clang … The sound was very loud and solid, so much so that at first I thought it must be a real bell. It had a resonant note as of metal yet the sound differed from any bell that I have ever heard as if the bell were cast of some metal we have not got. The sound had barely ceased when another bell clanged on a harmonizing note. In a little while I heard many bells … all up the road to Lough Bray. They clanged and answered each other. After some time those nearest ceased to sound and one by one the others left off so at last those still clanging were far off in the distance … this bell music ... obtruded itself with such force and was so <u>solid</u>, I find that I can remember it as I remember actual physical sounds.

[This ends the actual diary. The following was added later. Ed.]

28th June 1952: The perception of this music progresses by stages. In the first stage one is fascinated by the amazing strangeness, richness, the complicity of the music. The second stage builds into a pattern. It may be that of giant waves, each following but never over-taking the other, each with a running foam of melody on its crest; or the pattern may be that of a fountain, jetting upward and falling back upon itself; or, again, the pattern may follow that which a stone makes, thrown into a mountain tarn: circles widening on the still water. Sounds and vision are so inextricably blended that the sensation is not purely one of listening to music: the waves pass over and through one's consciousness, the fountain jets and falls, and one is part of it; the widening circles widen in oneself.

The third stage is one of spiritual perception.

In the fourth stage, which is pure ecstasy, there is nothing that the senses or the intellect can report on: since sound, colour, design, and spiritual perception become as it were the heart of a flame that leaves no residue.

UNCOLLECTED WRITINGS

This, and the piece that follows are both from The Irish Review *for 1911 and 1912.[3] The first is a curious piece, half short story and half personal memoir. It was later reprinted as part of* Flowering Dusk, *but this was its first appearance. It gives a powerful insight into the inner life of its author and should perhaps be read as a clear indication of her true feelings. It is also one of the best descriptions of the coming of a muse we have ever read. It is just possible that it refers to Maude Gonne, the celebrated Irish literary figure and mistress of W. B Yeats. The second piece has not been reprinted and is a review of W. E. Evans Wentz' seminal book* The Faery Faith in Celtic Countries. *The review contains some fascinating insights into Ella Young's understanding of the faery traditions. The third piece, from the* Oakland Tribune *for 1931 contains quotes from an interview with Ella. While in America, she was in high demand for lectures on Celtic mythology. Her lectures on faeries were always well received and often caused quite a stir! Of note in this interview are her views on children. How important these ideas are today as we see the urgency for reconnecting our youth to nature.*

THE ROSE QUEEN

I saw her when I was coming out of church. Church was hateful, but I had to go there. I sat through the hours of it resentfully pretending to myself that I did not see the blank walls or the dingy pulpit. The people looked ugly. I had a half-formed, childish suspicion that I looked ugly myself. It did not matter. Nothing mattered but the clock. If one counted the red velvet buttons on the pew-cushions, and the heads of the people who sat opposite, and the squares of glass in the window, and then looked cautiously back to the clock, the hand would have moved five minutes.

---

3   *Source: National Library of Ireland*

The hands of the clock had crawled through the last minute. The Benediction had been pronounced. I was escaping. How I hated the slow, shuffling crowd! People pressed upon me from behind; they pushed into the corridor in front of me; they swarmed on every side. It seemed hours before I came to the stairs leading from the gallery. The descent began – shuffling; hateful; intolerably slow. I was sick with rage. Beneath me I could see the mass that emptied itself into the vestibule through the central doors – a sluggish, monotonous, loathsomely-familiar ugliness, increasing every moment! I turned my face to the drab-painted wall and began to count the imitation bricks: I had counted them often before. One (I counted sullenly to myself) two – three – four – five – then some one laughed very softly and joyously, and looking down I saw Her. She was standing on the threshold of the outer door and she had laughed.

I did not think that any one could be so beautiful. She was like queens I had read about – queens of Avalon and Joyous Garde, beautiful as roses – I thought they had all been dead long ago.

Her hair was pure gold finely spun. Guinevere had hair of that colour, and the tallest of the queens who wept for Arthur in the boat, drifting on a sea without waves – a pale sea, milky white, coloured at the heart like an emerald.

She passed through the doorway and down the narrow entrance alley into the street. It seemed that no one wondered at her as she passed. I was the only one who knew – I and the queens in Avalon!

The house in which she lived had trees before it and long sloping lawns. A heavy iron gate shut it away from the rest of the world, and through the bars I could see a winding path with laurels on either side of it and great branching crimson roses.

It was an enchanted garden! The grass was very green and smooth as if it had been clipped that ladies might trail their cloaks of vair upon it. But no one ever came to gather the roses. A mysterious quiet was on the trees, a strange brightness on the leaves of the laurels. Perhaps they had been brought from a far country, and dreamed of stars no one else had seen; perhaps the witch, Vivien, had woven a spell about them, and quiet would hold them for ever as it held Merlin in the oak-wood of Broceliande. It was a marvellous hidden pleasaunce. I could believe almost that no one knew about it save myself: that no one ever walked there save the Rose-Queen.

She came upon me once as I thought of these things and stared at her roses. She came behind me, for she like myself was outside the gate.

"I see you love my roses," she said.

It was undreamt of and overwhelming. I began to move shamefacedly away.

"Do not go," she said. "I will give you a rose – only wait!"

I waited. She must have walked along the path where I had so often seen her in my thoughts but I do not know what she looked like among the laurels and roses or what she said when she came back and gave me the rose. It was only when she had gone that I knew my feet were in the white dust of the roadway and I had a rose in my hand – a rose from the enchanted garden! To me also, as to the Knights of the Siege Perilous, had come the Miraculous Happening.

Petal by petal the rose withered, yet the virtue of it remained with me and now I can always see the garden. It has grown larger: its lawns are like the lawns that stretch themselves between pale seas of gold in twilight skies, its roses are fiery-hearted like the dawn. I am not a child outside the gate any longer. I can go in now. The garden is so large that I have never come to the end of it. It is full of strange shadows and pale, beautiful light. The Rose-Queen is there faintly smiling, ivory-white, subtle as flame. She is as wise as the tallest of the queens in Avalon and in her hands which so many lovers have kissed she holds the million-petalled Rose of Dreams.

(*The Irish Review* Vol.1. June 1911, pp 187-189)

AN ANCIENT DOCTRINE

THE FAIRY FAITH IN CELTIC COUNTRIES By W. E. Evans Wentz, Oxford University Press.

Seldom has the Fairy-faith found an exponent so well fitted for the task as Doctor Wentz: thoroughly alive to the importance of the subject, he has spared neither time nor labour in the collection of his material, and to the investigation and arrangement of that material he brings a mind equipped with all the modern training and a heart that has not forgotten the wisdom of the early races.

It is perhaps this wisdom of the heart which makes him begin his book with a chapter on Environment, in which, speaking of Ireland and Brittany, he says:

"They have best preserved their old racial life in its simplicity and beauty with its high ideals, its mystical traditions, and its strong spirituality. And, curious though the statement may appear to some, this preservation of older manners and traditions does not seem to be due so much to geographical isolation as to subtle forces so strange and mysterious that to know them they must be felt: and their nature can only be suggested, for it cannot be described ... If anyone would know Ireland and test these influences – influences which have been so fundamental in giving to the Fairy-Faith of the past something more than mere beauty of romance and attractive form, something which even to-day, as in the heroic ages, is ever-living and ever-present in the centres where men of the second-sight say that they see fairies, in that strange state of subjectivity which the peasant calls Fairyland – let him stand on the Hill of Tara silently and alone at sunset, in the noonday, in the mist of a dark day. Let him silently and alone follow the course of the Boyne. Let him enter the silence of New Grange and of Dowth. Let him muse over the hieroglyphics of Lough Crew. Let him feel the mystic beauty of Killarney, the peacefulness of Glendalough, – of Monasterboise, of Clonmacnois, and the isolation of Arranmore."

The whole passage is too long for quotation, but in it is the name of Slieve Gullion, and of Moytura and Finvara, and Ben Bulben and Emain Macha – silent, powerful places to whom this oblation of acknowledgement is poured as fervently as Mathgen the Magician might have poured it when he asked the mountains and rivers and lakes of Ireland to help the Folk of Dana in their battle with the Fomor. Entering thus into the Celtic spirit, it is not surprising that Dr. Wentz has collected tales of Nairns and Corrigans and Pixies and Pookas; that he has talked with Seers versed in the mystery of the Spiritual Hierarchies, and that scholar and peasant alike has received him as comrade.

The collecting of this material from living witnesses-material which for many readers will form the most fascinating in the book was only part of the work Dr. Wentz set out to accomplish. He has ransacked the old Celtic MSS., and tales of to-day are compared with tales of one thousands years ago, and these again with stories from Egypt, India, and far-off Melanesia.

Having established the world-wide nature of belief in fairies, Dr. Wentz proceeds to consider various theories which have been put forward in explanation of this belief: he finds the "Pigmy Theory," the "Kidnap Theory" and the "Delusion" and "Imposture" theories inadequate, and so comes to the root idea of the book, the Celtic doctrine of the soul.

The Celts believed that the soul came out of a beautiful and undying world to manifest itself here through the medium of a body and returned again to that world from whence it might emerge many times and take each time a new earth-body. The soul was the real person, the body being only a cloak or mask; and, even whilst united to the body, the soul might go back to the divine world and converse with its comrades; this happened in vision or ecstasy, or when the body was in a deep trance, but in the old sagas mention is made of several who were rapt away in the body and, passing through the World of the Waters or Mid-world, came to the Honey-Plain, to the Land of the Living Heart, to the Land of the Ever-Young, and moved equal-fashion among gods until such time as they returned to tell folk in Ireland of their adventure. Crimthann, beloved of the Goddess Nair, brought back great treasure from Tir-nan-og (Land of the Ever-Young); Loegaire Liban, who, like Cuchulain, went to help the gods in a battle and took with him fifty noble warriors, returned with them to say farewell to his father and his clan. Riding on the white horses of Fairy-land, Loegaire and his comrades appeared before the assembly of the people of Connaught, who for a year had mourned him as dead. "Stay with us, Loegaire," cried his father, Crimthann Cass, "and I will give you the kingdom of the Three Connaughts, their gold and silver, their bridled horses, their beautiful damsels – do not refuse the gift." But Loegaire chanted a lay concerning the marvels of the other world, and said: "Marvellous it is, O Crimthann Cass, I was master of the Blue Sword – I would not give one night of the night of the gods for thy whole kingdom."

Cormac, son of Art, son of Conn the Hundred Fighter, entered the Land of Promise during his lifetime, and was shown many things in symbol by Mananaun, the Son of Lir, the god of Tir-nan-og. He saw the Fountain of Knowledge, "a shining fountain with five streams flowing out of it, and the hosts in turn a-drinking its water. Nine hazels of Buan grow over the well. The purple hazels drop their nuts into the fountain, and the five salmon which are in the fountain sever them and send their husks floating down the streams. Now, the sound of the falling of those streams is more melodious than any music that men sing." Concerning the Fountain, Mananaun said: "It is the Fountain of Knowledge, and the streams are the five senses through which knowledge is obtained. And no one will have knowledge who drinketh not a draught out of the fountain itself and out of the streams. The folk of many arts are those who drink of them both."

To drink of both streams – what a summing up of the Celtic ideal! To live magnificently, lavishly, to be strong-handed and wise-hearted, and sweet-spoken and fair, to look on and yet know life but a shadow, yet reach out and touch the Imperishable, the One. Perhaps Cormac did it – beautiful, triumphant, word-gifted Cormac, dead now so long ago and so nearly forgotten. But I do ill to pity him dead. What was death to the Celt but the-throwing-off of the body, the entrance untrammelled into life; were not all the Milesians Children of Bel the Un-Manifest, the Death-God, the Haughty Father, the Lord of the Ever-Living, and did not the world over which Bel ruled nourish and sustain this earth into which the souls of mountains and trees and rivers and the souls of men alike, descended as divine incursions?

"What is life?" asked a king of his druid. "It is the flight of a swallow through a raftered hall," said the druid. "What is life?" we ask the Celtic Myth-Makers; they reply: "The work of a god shaping the world." A brave faith this, and one that has not altogether perished with the centuries; some of it went to the making of Pelagian and other heresies, some of it lingers yet in the hearts of peasants who are scarce conscious of believing it, and some of it shapes to-day the creed of a few people who are not peasants – a few scholars and poets, who may perhaps be druids re-born. These are content to be silent, but a creed somewhat like their own has for years now been promulgated – in the European world, and even the readers of *Tit Bits* are familiar with the name of it – Theosophy.

"But what has all this to do with belief in fairies?" some sharp-witted person may ask. It has a good deal to do. Belief in fairies is, in the Celtic countries, mixed up with belief in the return of the souls of the dead and with belief in wonder-working stones and sacred wells; and with belief in the power of man, by prayer or penance or magic, to influence the unseen world, and this involves a conscious or unconscious belief in the Great Brotherhood which links stones and trees and man and animals and gods together by ties of the spirit. And so we come back again to the doctrine of the soul – for the soul in the Celtic belief is not a purely human possession; it belongs to all things, and all things exist because of it. This, if we want a learned phrase, is a pan-psychic view of the universe, and to such a view William James, most eminent and most modern of psychologists, seems to be feeling his way when he writes:

"Out of my experience, such as it is (and it is limited enough) one fixed conclusion dogmatically emerges, and that is this – that we with our lives are like islands in the sea, or like trees in the forest. The maple and the pine may whisper to each other with their leaves, and Connecticut and Newport hear each other's foghorns. But the trees also commingle their roots in

the darkness underground, and the islands also hang together through the ocean's bottom. Just so there is a continuum of cosmic consciousness, against which our individuality builds but accidental fences, and into which our several minds plunge as into a mother-sea or reservoir."

What do the other psychologists and metaphysicians and scientists think? It is an important question, and Dr. Wentz recognises its importance, for we are all sufficiently schooled now to know that if we want a really reliable opinion on any subject we must obtain it from a scientist. Dr. Wentz devotes a whole section of his book to a consideration of the attitude of modern science towards the Fairy-Faith, and he is able to sum up as follows:

"We conclude that the Other-world of the Celts and their Doctrine of Re-birth accord thoroughly in their essentials with modern science; and, accordingly, with other essential elements in the complete Fairy-Faith which we have in the preceding chapter found to be equally scientific, establish our Psychological Theory of the Nature and Origin of the Fairy-Faith upon a logical and solid foundation; and we now submit this study to the judgment of our readers ... Some beliefs which a century ago were regarded as absurdities are now regarded as fundamentally scientific. In the same way, what in this generation is heretical alike to the Christian theologian and to the man of science may in coming generations be accepted as orthodox."

These words end a very remarkable book; in collecting material for it, and following special courses of training and study, Dr. Wentz spent a number of years, and if he had polished his sentences and weighed his words as carefully as some of those amongst us do, he would have spent half a life-time in writing it. Every person who has not read the book would do well to buy or borrow a copy at once.

(*The Irish Review* Vol.2. August 1912, pp 313-316)

"ELVES AND FAIRIES CROWD INTO BERKELEY WITH POETESS" From *The Oakland Tribune*, September 22, 1931 p.1.

"It's fairy lore that makes the world beautiful ... there are fairies all about us, if we'll only look for them. How sad it is that a materialistic world laughs at them and their beauty ...

"If you want to develop imagination in a child, to fan the creative spark which may make him great, you can't restrict his thought. The fairy kingdom is a vast realm of magic where most anything can happen. It's a far more interesting place for a youngster than to take him riding in a street car ... Fairies, also, are not for all children, but to those who love them let them have them."

"...The modern child ... lives in a false world surrounded by mechanical toys and artificial amusements. There is no time to let the child sit and think; to turn out to nature, where the mountains, the birds and the flowers may talk to him – and they do talk – and to let him feel the beauty of things about him. And, then, how will a child know the greatest lessons of antiquity if his elders frown upon the rich folklore which affords him an inheritance of imagination and romance?"

Ella Young's cottage in Oceano, California, 2007.
Photograph by Denise Sallee

UNPUBLISHED & UNCOLLECTED POEMS

Ella Young left behind a number of uncollected and unpublished poems, most which are published here for the first time. The first appeared in the collection entitled Poems from New Songs: A Lyric Selection *(1904) which was edited by her then friend AE, with whom she subsequently fell out over political views. This is followed by five other poems, all previously unpublished, ending with a remarkable piece which was probably written only a few weeks before Ella Young's death. It stands as a fitting memorial to the work and life of this remarkable woman.*

A DREAM OF TIR-NAN-OGE

Without, a greyness floods the skies:
Within, a deeper greyness spares
All the pale twilight world that lies
Beyond my glimmering window squares.

I watch the gathering shadows creep
About the tree-tops, as of yore
We used to watch them, brooding deep
On some strange tale of faery lore.

The darkening branches move and sway,
The stars look through the dangled dusk
Thine eyes are there; I throw away
The years without thee, like a husk.

We are together, and o'erhead
The trees lean close to shut us in,
The giant trees whose branches spread
Back to the world where dreams begin.

O dim and deep this forest heart
And far away from haunts of pain:
Dream-fair its shadows meet and part:
The light comes through like golden rain.

There's golden apples on each bough;
The spreading branches gleam above.
Art thou, grown tall and queenly now,
The little maid I used to love?

The deep recesses are aglow
With purple and with pearl-pale green,
And all about thee come and go
Bright forms that bend and hail thee queen.

I know that now we stand within
The faery land of Heart's Delight,
Where old-time heroes came to win
The Spear, the Cup, the Sword of Might.

And thou are Naïve, the white flower
Of Death and Dream, of Hope and Doubt,
Immortal Beauty, for whose dower
The starry worlds were counted out.

Faint music softly swells and falls:
I follow thee, and we draw near
A deep where never storm-bird calls,
And thy boat waits us crystal clear.

Through shimmering seas of opal fire
We speed to gain the Well of Truth,
The Well that holds the World's Desire
And gives the Gods immortal youth.

Thy winged boat of diamond white,
Like a great bird that fain would fly,
Beats back in flakes of rainbow light
The crested waves swift fleeting by.

But ere we reach the magic Well
The glory fades across the seas;
A wind from earth revokes thy spell,
A wind that moans and stirs the trees;

I see their shadowy branches wave
Athwart my window in the gloom,
Scarce yet awake, while grey and grave
The light of morning fills the room.

Outside the sky is rose and gold
The dead moon slowly drifts away
My dream is done, for loud and bold
The dawn-lord sounds the trump of day.

ALCHEMY

(From the typed manuscript of *Smoke of Myrrh* – University of
California, Los Angeles, Special Collections)

To-night I weary of these narrow walls
That never held you! Let the adventure be
A winged galleon, purpling a sea
All sleep-enchanted, where the slow wave falls
In blossoms flame-bright, and no sea-bird calls
Athwart the deepening silence. Come with me,
Our galley waits us with sails shaken free:
We have no need of mariners or thralls.

Let us be going! Strange sea-foisoned beasts
Will eye us from the wave-slides. Sitting at feasts
In dim sea-palaces we'll hear the songs
Echoing from that foam-engirdled shore
Where the crowned Sirens lean for evermore
Lamenting lovers dead, and ancient wrongs.

PRINCE OF NIGHT
(From the typed manuscript of *Smoke of Myrrh* – University of
California, Los Angeles, Special Collections)

Wisdom I have, like those who are so wise
That they make bargain for it overnight
And have it from their birth-hour. So delight
That is but shadow-sooth, and sorrow dies.
No morn of Spring, no morning yet rise,
Will glad you on my threshold; nor will sight,
Sun-royal sight of you, make noontide bright:
Nor Hesper bring you with the darkening skies.

Fragile, alas, the world by dreaming won!
Perdurable, some alien world may be:
Let who will, vaunt its perils or its lures,
Make pattern of its stars, and mightier sun,
Despoil its jewelled empires, happily –
My world may perish, but the Dream endures!

PRINCE OF DAY
(From the typed manuscript of *Seed of the Pomegranate* – University of
California, Los Angeles, Special Collections)

White dawn before sunrise
Wherein the dawn star dies
When Helios lifts his head,
White dawn and ambient air
Let all the hours be fair
Since night's star-dust is shed:
Grant me this morn of May
For joyous holiday
Franked with thorn-blossom red.

TRYST AT EVEN-TIDE

(Written c.1956, shortly before Ella Young's death, in her correspondence
with Frances Clarke Sayers – University of California, Los Angeles,
Special Collections)

When I am dead
Morning will still be red
And Hesperius at eve
Lustre the skies.
No wind for me will grieve
Nor on my eyes
A dream lay finger light.

Beyond all need of sight
Or need of dream shut fast
Deep and more deep
My heart will sleep
With Earth's own heart at last.

ELLA YOUNG (1867-1956)
PUBLISHED WORKS

Prose

The Coming of Lugh, A Celtic-Wonder Tale. Illustrated by Maud Gonne. Dublin: Maunsel & Co., 1909.

Celtic Wonder-Tales. Illustrated by Maud Gonne. Dublin: Maunsel & Co., 1910.

The Wonder Smith and his Son: A Tale From the Golden Childhood of the World; retold by Ella Young. Illustrated by Boris Artzybasheff. New York, London: Longmans, Green & Co., 1927.

The Tangle-Coated Horse and Other Tales: Episodes From the Fionn Saga. Illustrated by Vera Bock. New York: Toronto: Longmans, Green and Co., 1929.

The Unicorn with Silver Shoes. Illustrated By Robert Lawson. New York: Longmans, Green & Co., 1932.

Flowering Dusk: Things Remembered Accurately and Inaccurately. New York: Toronto: Longmans, Green & Co., 1945.

In Translation

Récits de Mythologie Celtique, recueillis par Ella Young. Paris: Triades, 1962-1966.

Keltische Mythologie, aus dem Gälischen Nacherzählt. Aus dem Englischen übersetzt von Maria Christiane Benning. Ahrweiler/Rheinland: Are-Verlag, 1955.

El Caballo Recubierto de Maraña: y Otros Episodios de la Saga de Fionn McUail; illustraciones de Vera Bock; traducción Mónica Cumar y Juan Zegers. Santiago, Chile: Educiones Columba, 2002.

Poetry

In: AE. Ed. *New Songs. A Lyric Selection Made by A. E.* [i.e. George Russell.] from poems by Padraic Colum, Eva Gore-Booth, Thomas Keohler, Alice Milligan, Susan Mitchell, Seumas O'Sullivan, George Roberts, and Ella Young. Dublin: A. H. Bullen. London: O'Donoghue & Co., 1904.

Poems. Dublin: Maunsel & Co., 1906.

The Rose of Heaven: Poems. Illustrated by Maud Gonne. Dublin: Candle Press, 1920.

The Weird of Fionavar. Dublin: Talbot Press, 1922.

To the Little Princess: An Epistle San Francisco: Johnck and Seeger, 1930.

To Albert Bender: Saint Patrick's Night. San Francisco, Calif.: Grabhorn Press, 1934.

Marzilian, and other poems. Oceano, Calif.: Harbison & Harbison, c.1938.

Seed of the Pomegranate, and other poems. [Privately published, 1949].

ABOUT THE EDITORS

JOHN MATTHEWS

John Matthews is an historian, folklorist and author. He has been a full time writer since 1980 and has produced over ninety books on the Arthurian Legends and Grail Studies, as well as short stories and a volume of poetry. He has devoted much of the past thirty years to the study of Arthurian Traditions and myth in general. His best known and most widely read works are *Pirates* (Carlton/Atheneum), No 1 children's book on the *New York Times Review* best-seller list for 22 weeks in 2006, *The Grail, Quest for Eternal Life* (Thames & Hudson, 1981) *The Encyclopaedia of Celtic Wisdom* (Element, 1994) and *The Winter Solstice* (Quest Books, 1999) which won the Benjamin Franklin Award for that year. His book *Celtic Warrior Chiefs* was a New York Public Library recommended title for young people.

John has been involved in a number of media projects, as an advisor and contributor, including an animated Arthurian TV series, a film about the magical defence of Britain during the 2nd World War, and *The Real Merlin* for Channel 4. In 2003 he was the historical advisor to the Jerry Bruckheimer movie King Arthur, and has made appearances on both History Channel and Discovery Channel specials on Arthur and the Holy Grail.

DENISE SALLEE

Denise Sallee is a California historian, with a graduate degree from the University of California, Los Angeles and a visual artist. Denise is the author of *Daughters of Time*, a novel for young adults, and is currently working on three screenplays. She lives on the Central Coast of California.

PRAISE FOR ELLA YOUNG

"Thank you many times for your stories. Both are interesting and the one about the fight for the harvest is really of great importance." **W.B. Yeats to Ella Young, 1903.**

"I often read your Wonder Tales, no one has ever written of those old stories as you did, or made them as living…" **Maud Gonne to Ella Young, 1943.**

"The freshness of the morning, a clean wind, and a clear sky." **James Stephens on her poetry.**

"She interprets the great cycles of Gaelic story-telling as no one else can." **Pronnseas O Suilleabhain, Lecturer on Irish and English in the University of Freiburg, Baden, Germany.**

"Ella Young is one of Ireland's real artists. For years she has lectured on the myth and folk-lore and Celtic tradition. She is one of the most picturesque personalities that the Irish Renaissance has given us…" ***The Gael*, May 1922.**

"Her Celticism comes to her from both Ireland and Scotland. And all her life she has been devoted to the far places where Celtic tradition is still full…she knows the lore of these places. A scholar, too, she is well read in the heroic and mystical literatures of all other lands…Her deep conviction about the destiny of Ireland gives strength to her story-telling…Ella Young knows the pattern of the Gaelic stories, and she can reproduce it in a way that has charm and freshness. She writes a prose that has in it the sense of things see, and that is swiftly moving at the same time." **Padraic Colum:** ***Ella Young: An Appreciation.***

"There is a spell upon her prose, a real enchantment, that echoes through the mind like remembered music…to read the prose books of Ella Young… is to move in a world of epic proportion, heroic deed and heroic character, set against a background of warm earth, where even the gods delight in the small intimacy of blossom and flower…These tales are told with great conviction, as if they were rooted in the experience of the storyteller." **From Frances Clarke Sayers (Noted American librarian and authority on children's literature.)**

www.ingramcontent.com/pod-product-compliance
Lightning Source LLC
Chambersburg PA
CBHW030321020726
47493CB00004B/1117